Poe…

Motion

Shropshire

Edited by Annabel Cook

Young Writers
First published in Great Britain in 2004 by:
Young Writers
Remus House
Coltsfoot Drive
Peterborough
PE2 9JX
Telephone: 01733 890066
Website: www.youngwriters.co.uk

SB ISBN 1 84460 405 5

Foreword

This year, the Young Writers' 'Poetry In Motion' competition proudly presents a showcase of the best poetic talent selected from over 40,000 up-and-coming writers nationwide.

Young Writers was established in 1991 to promote the reading and writing of poetry within schools and to the youth of today. Our books nurture and inspire confidence in the ability of young writers and provide a snapshot of poems written in schools and at home by budding poets of the future.

The thought effort, imagination and hard work put into each poem impressed us all and the task of selecting poems was a difficult but nevertheless enjoyable experience.

We hope you are as pleased as we are with the final selection and that you and your family continue to be entertained with *Poetry In Motion Shropshire* for many years to come.

Contents

The Poems

Fat Lady Countdown

Seven fat dinner ladies
Cooking spotted dicks
One forgot the custard
Then there were six

Six fat dinner ladies
Risking children's lives
Accidentally killed one
Then there were five

Five fat dinner ladies
Cooking chicken raw
Gave it to the children
Then there were four

Four fat dinner ladies
Bursting for a wee
Took too long
Then there were three

Three fat dinner ladies
Got water from the loo
A boy got poisoned
Then there were two

Two fat dinner ladies
Cooking up some scones
Didn't cook them correctly
Then there was one

One fat dinner lady
Thought she was a hero
Got too big-headed
Then there were zero.

Andy Care (13)

Storm

Splish, splash, the rain flies down,
Boom, bang, the thunder echoes around,
Flash, bash, the lightning goes *crash*,
Clitter-clatter, the rain goes *patter*
On my window ledge and
Tiles hanging off the edge.
It's dark and no one's in the park,
Swish, swish, the wind shakes the bush.
Twirl, twirl, a tornado attacks and sears over the piers.
Bang, clang, the waves crash
And ships are bashed
On the rocks,
Drip, drop, the rain drips into my socks.
Howl, yowl, animals bark and shout,
Watch out there's a storm about!

Lee Evans (13)
Abraham Darby School

A Winter's Night

The snow fell silently on a cold winter's night,
It covered the houses and all the ground,
It glistened like silver and flecks of white,
As the moon shone and the stars did shine,
There was peace and quiet, not even a sound.

The animals hid all snug and warm,
Cuddled in families under a mound,
Waiting for the spring to be born,
The wind did blow up above,
As the snow fell silently on the ground.

Michael Edwards (11)
Abraham Darby School

Countdown

Seven fat dinner ladies
Doing cooking tricks
One got lost
Then there were six

Six fat dinner ladies
Boiling things live
One jumped out
Then there were five

Five fat dinner ladies
Walking through the door
One got stuck
Then there were four

Four fat dinner ladies
One needs a wee
Couldn't get there quick enough
Then there were three

Three fat dinner ladies
Making a stew
One tripped over
Then there were two

Two fat dinner ladies
Talking to their mums
The other walked off
Then there was one

One fat dinner lady
Set up a bomb
The school was blown up
Then there were none.

Louise Hanley (12)
Abraham Darby School

Abraham Darby School

A larm clock goes off,
B reakfast on the table,
R eady for school
A nd ready to learn
H alfway to school, a stop for the shops
A nd back on the way
M any people say good morning.

D etentions for the badly behaved
A nd merits for the good.
R ooftops stand tall in the brightness of sun,
B uildings around the area look small unlike the school.
Y et when you leave, it looks small.

S chool is over,
C heering people run across the road.
H ead of school stays late at night.
O r maybe on a Saturday she might visit the school,
O r even stay in bed,
L ater that day you think, *shall I do my homework?*

Shane Payne (11)
Abraham Darby School

Bullies

If you bully, you're not fair,
All the people can hardly bear,
Don't laugh at what they wear,
How they dress or do their hair,
You should be polite and share a smile
Once in a while
Give a grin, show your chin
Laugh and joke, *never* smoke
Be nice and smile once in a while.

Katherine Bates (12)
Abraham Darby School

That's Me, Tiff G

I stay up late
I throw my plate
I watch the telly
And smell a welly
That's me, Tiff G

I wake up in the morn
I see a bull's horn
I shout and yell
Some people wished I would go to Hell
That's me, Tiff G

I spit and chew
I throw a person's shoe
I once read a book
I really didn't look
That's me, Tiff G

I go to bed at 3 o'clock
I really don't want to wear that smock
I throw my covers and my sheets
At school they are cheats
That's me, Tiff G

It's school time now
I don't know how
I don't like school
They think they're cool
That's me, Tiff G

Now my mum can calm me down
Please, please she needs a crown
Let me grow
And then I'll know.
That's me, Tiff G.

Tiffany Greenwood (12)
Abraham Darby School

Me

I scream and shout
I stand and stare
I couldn't really care
I'm always there walking about

I throw a plate
I mouth my mate
I go on dates

I'm never good
I pick a bud

Don't shout at me
You'll be stung by a bee
I'll chuck my book
I'm so stuck

I've had no luck
Don't look at me
Soon you'll see this is me

Now my mum has helped me out
I will be as good as gold

I'll never scream
I'll never shout
I'll never ever chuck a book
So you're in luck.

Hailey Hamer (11)
Abraham Darby School

Stan

There was a young man from Japan
Who sat on the roof of a van
The van shot off very fast
He fell off with a blast
That was goodbye to young man Stan.

Sophie Linkins (11)
Abraham Darby School

Naughty Matthew

This boy always had to punch
He always had to crunch
Pulled girls' hair
And made it tear
It was Naughty Matthew

Matthew made all the girls cry
As he always ate their apple pie
They told Miss
But he took no notice
It was always Naughty Matthew

He always had to cheat at games
And kept on doing the same
He always won
And made a ton
It was Naughty Matthew

His mum told him, 'I love you too'
He said, 'I'll flush you down the loo'
She said it twice
Then got covered in mice
It was Naughty Matthew

He always got invited to his friend's dance
But he always put him in his pants
His friend said, 'Come'
So he gave him some
It was always Naughty Matthew

They put him out of the school gang
As they always called him guard hang
He gave them a bang
That made them go tang
It was Naughty Matthew.

Matthew Bethell (11)
Abraham Darby School

Ghosts

Ghosts come out at night
And give children a fright,
They sit up in their bed,
Cuddling their teddy and screaming.

The ghosts get bored,
They get another score,
That makes ninety-nine,
They walk through the wall
And across the garden on the washing line.

Mum came running,
Her child is humming,
Trying to calm himself down,
Mum says, 'You clown,
You made me shiver,
You've cried a river,
I can tell you were scared,
Now let's do our prayers.

We will talk in the morning
Hope it's not boring
I won't have time
I've got to fix my chime

Tonight you will rest
And don't be a pest
You will get sleep
Nothing will creep
I will let
You have a pet
In the morning.'

Hannah Paskin (11)
Abraham Darby School

The Dancing Angels

Seven dancing angels
Practising their tricks
One did a disappearing act
Then there was six

Six dancing angels
Looking at the butterflies
One tried to catch it
Then there were five

Five dancing angels
Running to the door
One banged into it
Then there were four

Four dancing angels
Having a cup of tea
One cup was too hot
So then there were three

Three dancing angels
One lost its shoe
That one went looking for it
Then there were two

Two dancing angels
Watching a beautiful swan
The swan pecked at the angel
So then there was one

One dancing angel
Shouting at the swan
The swan gave it a wish to go to Earth
So then there were none.

Maisie Pugh (12)
Abraham Darby School

Jack And The Beanstalk

Once there lived a boy named Jack
Who lived in a very tumbled down shack
He had no food and he had no money
So every day he played with a bunny

One day Jack's mother said
'I'm sorry, Jack, you have to be fed
You'll have to go sell Daisy
Unless you want to go crazy'

Jack lead his cow down the path
And met a man who needed a bath
Suddenly they could not be seen
And they left Jack holding a single bean

Jack ran to bed
And then he said
'You're mean'
But Mum threw the bean

Mum and Jack had a talk
And then they noticed a beanstalk
Jack turned the key
And shouted, 'I'll be back for tea'

Jack ran quick
Then into a skip
The giant was behind him
And his name was Tim

Jack split the bean
So nothing could be seen
And they spent all their money
And bought lots of honey.

Clementina Warner (11)
Abraham Darby School

Seven Fat Dinner Ladies

Seven fat dinner ladies
Building a house of bricks
The house collapsed
Then there were six

Six fat dinner ladies
One hadn't arrived
She did not come
Then there were five

Five fat dinner ladies
Cleaning the floor
One slipped up
Then there were four

Four fat dinner ladies
One got stung by a bee
One went home
Then there were three

Three fat dinner ladies
One had the flu
Stayed at home
Then there were two

Two fat dinner ladies
One was a con
She got the sack
Then there was one

One fat dinner lady
Playing in the sun
She got burnt
Then there were none.

Toni Griffiths (12)
Abraham Darby School

O My Little Sister

O my little sister
You really cannot miss her
She skips and jumps round everywhere
With her big green spiky hair

Her hair is always in a mess
She'd never wear a frilly dress
She never eats human food
She's always in that playful mood
O my little sister

O my little sister
She never goes to bed at night
At school she's always in a fight
At weekends she's always watching telly
My mum says her brain will turn to jelly

Her bedroom's always in a tip
Really it should be in the skip
All my friends think she's mad
Though really she's not that bad
O my little sister

She says that she's from far away
Even though she wants to stay
Her true home is by the moon
Maybe she'll go back soon
O my little sister.

Hannah White (12)
Abraham Darby School

Was I Worth It?

Near to the door
he paused to stand
as he took his class ring
off her hand.
All who were watching
did not speak
as a silent tear
ran down his cheek
and through his mind
the memories ran
of the moments they walked
and ran in the sand (hand in hand).
But now her eyes were so terribly cold
as he would never again
have her to hold
they all watched in silence
as he bent near
and whispered the words . . .
I love you in her ear.
He touched her face and started to cry
as he put on his ring and wanted to die
and just then the wind began to blow
as they lowered her casket into the snow.
This is what happens to man alive
when friends let friends drink and drive.

Kelly Stratten (14)
Abraham Darby School

Tiny Disco Dancers Countdown Poem

Seven tiny disco dancers
Dancing to Phixx
One fell in
Then there were six

Six tiny disco dancers
Watching a hive
One got stung
Then there were five

Five tiny disco dancers
Trying to bore
One lost her voice
Then there were four

Four tiny disco dancers
Standing by a tree
One ran away
Then there were three

Three tiny disco dancers
Cleaning the crew
One fell in
Then there were two

Two tiny disco dancers
Planting a bomb
One blew up then
There was one

One tiny disco dancer
Was staring at the sun
She went blind
Then there were none.

Kirsty Flanigan (12)
Abraham Darby School

Countdown

Seven stupid children
Fighting with sticks
One went too far
Then there were six

Six stupid children
Playing with a beehive
One got stung
Then there were five

Five stupid children
Kicking at the door
One broke their foot
Then there were four

Four stupid children
Drinking water out of the sea
One started choking
Then there were three

Three stupid children
Went to the loo
One started a fight
Then there were two

Two stupid children
Think that swearing's fun
One got told off
Then there was one

One stupid child
Having too much fun
But he went too far
Then there were none!

Laura Coleman (13)
Abraham Darby School

A Ghost

A ghost goes haunting in a house,
When he was haunting he found a little mouse,
Along the hallway up and down,
Outside in the swimming pool he tried to drown,
Nobody knows why he did this,
A ghost goes *hiss, hiss, hiss.*

A ghost goes haunting every night,
In its long cloak of white,
Along the corridor bright and high,
Outside there is a moonlit sky,
Nobody knows why he is here,
A ghost goes haunting very near.

A ghost goes haunting very near,
Although he's a ghost, he still has fears.
Along the room's creaky floor,
Outside there is a squeaky door,
Nobody knows why he's lost his fear,
A ghost goes and watches the fog clear.

Lauren Baldi (11)
Abraham Darby School

Quietly And Noisily

Quietly the crook broke in
Quietly he started to begin
Quietly he went up the stair
Quietly he ate a pear
Quietly he stole more and more
Quietly he crept out of the door

Noisily the police chased him
Noisily he jumped into a bin
Noisily the police looked round
Noisily a clue was found
Noisily he was caught by PC Snail
Noisily he was put in jail.

Lee Campbell (12)
Abraham Darby School

The Phantom!

If you want me to flick the lights
And slam your bedroom door

If you want me to ring the phone
And stamp upon the floor

Then wish for me with all your might
And whisper this three times at night
The phantom!
The phantom!
The phantom!

If you want me to haunt your house
And walk through the tall walls

If you want me to shake your bed
And make some deathly calls

Then wish for me with all your might
And whisper this three times at night
The phantom!
The phantom!
The phantom!

Jodie Sykes (12)
Abraham Darby School

Me And My Brother

When I was 9, my brother and I went skiing in the snow,
He showed me what to do,
My brother thought *go on have a go*,
Suddenly he went blue,
I started off, then I fell down into a tree
And my brother sighed *oh no!*
The snow was very slippery and cold,
My brother said, 'What a roll.'

Elly Willets (11)
Abraham Darby School

The Phantom! -But My Version

If you want me to walk through walls
And blow wind through your hair
If you want me to ring your phone
And give you a scare

Then wish for me three times at night
The phantom!
The phantom!
The phantom!

If you want me to flicker your lights
And whisper things in your ear
If you want me to shake your bed
And then you'll know I'm here

Then wish for me three times at night
The phantom!
The phantom!
The phantom!

Becky Hayfield (12)
Abraham Darby School

The Sea

I thought a life at sea
Would be for me
Doing as the sailors do
So one day
I ran away
The nearest ship to seek
But life at sea
Is not for me
It only made me
Sick!

Craig Green (12)
Abraham Darby School

Countdown

Seven fat dinner ladies
Put in some sticks
One got caught
Then there were six

Six fat dinner ladies
Found a beehive
One got stung
Then there were five

Five fat dinner ladies
Broke the kitchen door
One fell over
Then there were four

Four fat dinner ladies
Having a cup of tea
One dropped a mug
And then there were three

Three fat dinner ladies
All called Sue
One got married
Then there were two

Two fat dinner ladies
All the children gone
One went with them
And then there was one

One fat dinner lady
Thought it was fun
Ate all the puddings
Then there were none.

Scott Merricks (12)
Abraham Darby School

Spells

(Inspired by 'Macbeth' by William Shakespeare)

Round about the cauldron go:
In the poisoned entrails throw -
In they go the dead man's toes,
A wrinkly, old spotted nose,
Pour them in, the dandruff flakes,
Crusted earwax and bogey cakes!
Add to the flavour smelly socks,
Lumps of mouldy gum as it rots!
A chunk of bloodstained horror story,
Lots of drama, blood and glory.
Suck it in, the smelly spit and snot,
Mix it in the evil flowing pot.
Grime and dirt from under broken nails,
Buy one get one free slimy snails.
I wonder what this will make?
Something vile, give the grime a shake!

Emily Ramsay (12)
Abraham Darby School

Summer Lunchtimes

On summer lunchtimes in the playground,
Girls walk aimlessly,
Shirts flutter in a gentle breeze,
Ice cream drips from a soft cone.
The sun beats down,
With reds, yellows and oranges,
Sweat seeps from boys' brows,
As bees buzz by a full bloomed flower,
Happy children playing games,
Hopscotch,
Football
And skipping rhymes,
Singing and laughing sweep the ground,
Golden buds in a lush green river,
Could life like this ever end?

Kirsty Hamilton (12)
Abraham Darby School

My Best Friend

My friend Jo and I would play
Round each other's every day,
We played in the garden, we played in the park,
We stayed out late, until it went dark.
We like the same music, we like the same food,
If we weren't together, we would be in a mood.
I can still remember that awful day,
When her mum told me they were moving away,
I couldn't believe those words she said,
They echoed round and round my head.
I felt sick, my legs turned to jelly,
I got a funny feeling in my belly.
They couldn't leave, they couldn't go,
I would miss my best friend, Jo.
But they left for their new home
And left me here all alone!
But now I've got a new mate,
My friend, Kate!

Jodi Stansfield (12)
Abraham Darby School

When You Die

When you die
I know where you go
Angel wings
And glistening snow

When you die
I know where you fly
Sunny things
And a beautiful sigh

When you die
I know where you lie
Golden halos
And a sweet plum pie.

Holly Goldie (11)
Abraham Darby School

Without You I'm Like . . .

Without you I'm like . . .
A bird with no wings
A girl with no hair
A world with no kings
A test that isn't fair

Without you I'm like . . .
A bird with no perch
A dog with no ears
A vicar with no church
A person with no fears

Without you I'm like . . .
A person with no spine
A dog with no bone
A snail with no slime
A piano with no tone

Without you I'm like . . .
A flower with no petal
A TV with no sound
A car with no metal
A ball that's not round

Without you I'm like . . .
A plant with no root
A car with no oil
A horn with no toot
A kettle that don't boil

Without you I'm like . . .
A person with no clothes
An icicle with no snow
A dog with no nose
A wind with no blow.

Sarah Smith (11)
Abraham Darby School

Seven Little Footballers

Seven little footballers
One had a pick 'n' mix
He got fat
Then there were six

Six little footballers
One took a dive
He saw red
Then there were five

Five little footballers
Ready to score
He fell over
Then there were four

Four little footballers
One forgot his key
He went home
Then there were three

Three little footballers
One lost most of his crew
He decided to go
Then there were two

Two little footballers
One planted a bomb
He was arrested
Then there was one

One little footballer
He had gone
To his house
Then there were none.

Dean Ridley (12)
Abraham Darby School

Simply Summer

On summer mornings in the playground,
The girls stand still,
Their warm hands spread
In the summer air.

The warm air gently blows
About the playground
And the warmth gives an urge for water
And stretches in the tender skin.

The occasional gulp of water,
Sound long and loud,
And the sun burns red,
The flowers blooming out.

I take my bottle
Into my sweaty hands,
Take a gulp,
Then a sip

And enjoy the summer's day.

James Hill (12)
Abraham Darby School

The Seaside

I sit sunbathing on my chair,
As children scream
And run around nearly bare.
The splash of the sea,
As people play
And have picnics for tea.
The rolling of the pebbles,
As they swish to and fro,
Children acting like little rebels,
Girls walking round in swimming cosies tight,
Murmur of the children,
As it is becoming night.

Toni Nicholls (12)
Abraham Darby School

The Beach

I've been to the beach once,
Though I remember all,
This is what I saw:

Four tall lifeguards
Looking for a drowning person,
Billions of people
Minding their business,
Some were swimming,
Some were sunbathing,
I'd never seen so many people
All in one place.

I saw sandcastles
Made by the little children,
The waves were high,
So I never got into the water.

Vongai Mazorodze (12)
Abraham Darby School

Untitled

Mobile, mobile
Ringing all the time
Mobile, mobile
Who is on the line?

Phone, phone
You don't leave me alone
I'm always hearing my flashy ring tone

Texts, texts
You're making me vex
Texts, texts
Who's sending me one next?

Ian Hamilton (12)
Abraham Darby School

From Beast To Feast

(Inspired by 'Macbeth' by William Shakespeare)

Round about the cauldron go;
In the poisoned entrails throw -
A fox's spleen
And frogs' bones clean,
A crusty toenail
And ants impaled,
A small pig's tongue,
Dead man's lung,
A large bat wing
And an opera song-sing,
Demon's broth,
An old dead moth,
A tiny fish
And an unlucky wish,
Double, double, toil and trouble,
Fire burn and cauldron bubble,
Turn this man
From beast
To feast.

Hannah Cogings (13)
Abraham Darby School

Sunshine

The sun is shining by the seaside,
I lick my lollipop
And play on the slide,
I run around and swim in the sea,
I like to play hide-and-seek with my brother, Lee,
What a lovely day it's been,
Buzz, buzz,
I've just got stung by a bee.

Jade Ferris (12)
Abraham Darby School

The Phantom!

If you want me to move your bed
And flicker all the light
If you want me to creak the floor
And make you scream with fright

Then wish for me with all your might
And whisper this three times at night
The phantom!
The phantom!
The phantom!

If you want me to make things move
And keep you wide awake
If you want me to creak your floorboards
And make your bedroom shake

Then wish for me with all your might
And whisper this three times at night
The phantom!
The phantom!
The phantom!

Nicole MacArthur (11)
Abraham Darby School

Storm

It's a dark, cold night
People lying in bed trying to get to sleep
Hearing the pitter-patter of raindrops
Pitter-patter, pitter-patter
Bang, crash, thud
A storm had broke in the wind whistling against the trees
Rain dripping off rooftops
It thudded against the floor, the wind breaking the fence
Then it stopped, pitter-patter, pitter-patter.

Daniel Hamer (12)
Abraham Darby School

Seven Little Gymnasts

Seven little gymnasts
Eating their pick 'n' mix
One threw up
And then there were six

Six little gymnasts
Went for a dive
One girl drowned
And then there were five

Five little gymnasts
Walking through the door
One smacked her head
And then there were four

Four little gymnasts
Swimming in the sea
One was eaten by a shark
And then there were three

Three little gymnasts
With shoes incredibly new
One broke the heel
Then there were two

Two little gymnasts
Shelly and Sharon
One went home sick
Then there was one

One little gymnast
Where have the rest gone?
She went home
And then there were none.

Sophie Coley (12)
Abraham Darby School

Disco Dancers

Seven sparkly disco dancers
Doing magic tricks
One did something wrong
Then there were six

Six sparkly disco dancers
Haven't yet arrived
One went totally mental
Then there were five

Five sparkly disco dancers
All walked to the door
One got stuck
Then there were four

Four sparkly disco dancers
Were looking so glee
One was too late
Then there were three

Three sparkly disco dancers
Were waiting for you
One was ill
Then there were two

Two sparkly disco dancers
Were watching John
One went shopping
Then there was one

One sparkly disco dancer's
Hair was in a bun
One went home
Then there were none.

Chloe Jones (12)
Abraham Darby School

Fat Dinner Ladies

Seven fat dinner ladies
One changed her mix
She lost her job
Then there were six

Six fat dinner ladies
One did not arrive
They found out she was sick
Then there were five

Five fat dinner ladies
One got hit by a door
Her nose burst out with blood
Then there were four

Four fat dinner ladies
They found out she was he
He got a new job
Then there were three

Three fat dinner ladies
One went, 'Moo'
She turned into a cow
Then there were two

Two fat dinner ladies
One went home with her mum
She never came back to work
Then there was one

One fat dinner lady
Went and scared John
He took her to the club
Now there were none.

David Jones (12)
Abraham Darby School

Seven Small Dancers

Seven small dancers
Trying to do tricks
One hurt themselves
And then there were six

Six small dancers
Doing the jive
One got fired
And then there were five

Five small dancers
Tapping on the floor
One fell over
And then there were four

Four small dancers
Dancing free
One got caught
Then there were three

Three small dancers
Didn't have a clue
One thought of something
And then there were two

Two small dancers
Five of them gone
The other got stage fright
Then there was one

One small dancer
Dancing on his own
There was no use
And then there were none.

Michelle Hill (12)
Abraham Darby School

Seven Little Devils

Seven little devils
All having fits
One of them died
Then there were six

Six little devils
All having a dive
One of them choked
Then there were five

Five little devils
Breaking the law
One got arrested
Then there were four

Four little devils
Eating their tea
One started a food fight
Then there were three

Three little devils
All playing boo!
One got scared
Then there were two

Two little devils
One named Ron
He had a heart attack
Then there was one

One little devil
Thought he was a hero
But he was defeated
Then there were zero.

Liam Preece (12)
Abraham Darby School

Disco Dancers!

Seven little disco dancers
Dancing by burning candle wicks
One got burned
Then there were six

Six little disco dancers
Feeling so alive
One bumped their head
Then there were five

Five little disco dancers
Taking a tour
One tripped up
Then there were four

Four little disco dancers
Waiting for the tea
One felt so ill
Then there were three

Three little disco dancers
They went to see their mum
Two never came back
Then there was one

One little disco dancer
Being a hero
She tripped to the ground
Then there were zero.

Hannah Morris (12)
Abraham Darby School

The Phantom

If you want me to flicker the lights
And sway through your bedroom walls

If you want me to creak the gate
And ring the phone for calls

Well then wish this three times a night
The phantom, the phantom, the phantom . . .

If you want me to shake the floor
And whisper your name out

If you want me to carry steel chains
And throw your bed about

Well then wish this three times a night
The phantom, the phantom, the phantom.

Oliver Rimmer (11)
Abraham Darby School

The Owl

Owl, owl, in the tree
Why do you sit there staring at me?
Big wide eyes, soft brown feathers,
That will keep you warm in all different weathers.

Your oily coat that keeps you dry,
With your silent wings when you fly so high,
You swoop down in search of prey,
Breaking their back bones if they get in your way.

You do not blink, you only stare,
You have no eyelids, they're not there,
With 14 bones as you turn your head
And you wake up whilst we are in bed.

So goodbye Mr Owl up in that tree,
Now I know why you sit there staring at me.

Ricky Welch (12)
Abraham Darby School

Myself

I have blue eyes and blonde hair
In addition, I can never sit still in my chair
I have loads of friends
When we break up, we all make amends

I go to the Abraham Darby School
Which I think is cool
We have five lessons in a day
I'd never change schools, no way

I have two sisters, one younger and one older
My big sister always makes me carry her folder
She's in Year 10, doing her coursework
On it, her boyfriend is such a jerk

I am in Year 8
I'm always with a mate
My tutor's name is Miss Stack
I bet she would like to give kids a smack.

Lorissa Weaver (12)
Abraham Darby School

Owls

I fly by night,
I am always silent,
You don't know where I'll hit,
You don't know where I am,
My eyes watch you like a beam,
I won't get you out my sight,
When I fly down
Ready to strike,
You will not hear me,
Bang!
Silence,
There is no sound.

Aaron Simpson (12)
Abraham Darby School

The Deliverer

My wheels burn against the chilled,
dead road. 6am tranquillity in
all respects. Here comes the
Royal Mail. I'm the royal
bearer of good news
BAD N3W5

You should be ashamed with net curtains that dirty

John St Maria's Ave. Fly by. Such backward
Holy places. Nos 1, 3, 5, 7, 9: score.
Letterboxes snap as they gobble
printed food. Swallow that
smug tax bill like a
50UR P1LL

Does he know you're screwing the milkman to pay it off?

Mrs A Bowen waits for her Guardian. Her
black and white dog waits for me. I wait
for a promotion. Tenerife. How
nice. Postcodes on postcards
in the future please
MY D3AR

Is it Alison or Andrea? Anne's don't drink semi-skimmed

So needed yet so under appreciated. We steal
the free shampoo samples out of spite.
First class failure. His weary face
smears off the brass box as
I move along. Odds
TH3N 3VEN5

Mr S T Ranger has many secrets, but I'm not one to share

I don't get many letters of my own these days. I'm
a postman. I'm the postman. I am postman.
It's a job. To live. To post the
world away. It could
B3 W0R53.

Ben Bransfield (16)
Adams' Grammar School

Revenge!

It's their fault that I do these crazy things,
Not mine. They shouldn't have died when I was so young
And left me in that orphanage. Traitors. They left me on my own
To grow up. Now they must pay through the pain of other families.
They must pay through their suffering.

I hate it when I see them. A loving family,
Together, enjoying themselves. I go for families with a single child,
Like I was. I study them, make sure they like each other,
Care for each other. Love. I wait for them, till they are together.
Follow them. Then when the time is right, I make my move.

I wait till the child is alone. I take him,
Blindfold him and hide him. The parents worry. Next,
I do the same with the mother. Let her reunite with her son.
Rejoice. Then it's the father,
Now I have all three.

I wait till late, till dark and then take them down to the river,
'This is where it all ends,' I say to the child and laugh.
I tie the parents together face to face. One last look. Then,
I put the stones in the bag and tie it round their feet. I drag
Them into the river to let them drown and shout, 'See ya
Mum and Dad.'

I let the child witness it all. See his parents meeting their
inevitable death.
Watch the tears well up in his eyes. Despair. Then,
I blindfold him again and leave him to be found.
Leave him to go to the horrible orphanage.
Get horrible new parents.

I leave the scene and
Prepare for my next victims. Prepare,
For the next lives to be ruined. Just like mine was.
Make another child suffer. Just like I did. Next is my thirteenth family.
Revenge.

Kieran Dunphy (16)
Adams' Grammar School

Free?

I often wonder how it would feel to fly,
Like a bird, high above the clouds.
All emotions are lost as I soar . . .
Twenty-two stitches.
To feel the wind in my hair,
You say you love me but you do it again.

Finally free.
The time you banged my head against the wall.
I burnt the dinner,
Battered.
Beaten.
Bruised.
Scared for life some might say.

Too many chances. Broken promises.
'Let this be a lesson,' you said.
To love and to cherish was the oath we swore . . .

It's not your fault they said, self defence.
When I told them what I'd done,
What I felt like when I put the gun to his head
And pulled the trigger. Dead.
On the kitchen floor in a river of blood, I cried.

Elizabeth Zofia Siarkiewicz (16)
Adams' Grammar School

Orpheus

The cuts used to bring a smile to my lips;
An artist signs his work, and you left your mark on me.
You said you were drawn to the purity in me.
'Little Boy Lolita', you called me.
Bath.

I came from a life just as dark as yours;
unwanted by my family, undesired by my generation.
The crowd was a sanctuary for me,
a darkling throng of heat and want. You saw me.
Razor.

Leaving our lives behind, we became creatures of the night;
angels of the underworld. Shackles to shackles.
You said our love was true, that it would always burn.
And it will - until there is nothing left.
Music.

The blood wells up as I press down, clouding out as I lower my arm.
My head falls back into a river of scarlet visions,
this Styx absolves me of my sins, draining them from my body.
Finally, I have what you could never give.
Escape.

Philip Ellis (16)
Adams' Grammar School

Chloroform

Return, single, return. Please.
A glance, gaze, cheers, but
they don't know me, don't
notice the man before them, who

darts, skips, dances on the
night. Chloroform. I laugh.
Ignorance.

Bliss. I check the mirror,
they smile, game,
'Have a pleasant journey.'
But in my mind I

lacerate them, tear them,
I taste them.

'Have a pleasant journey.'
I've killed them all before.

Robin Andrews (16)
Adams' Grammar School

Stranger

The sea of black surrounding me
Very fitting for the occasion
I gather it's a funeral
The sobbing sounds of grieving people
This person's very missed

'Excuse me please . . . I said excuse me please'
Grievance does not incur rudeness!
All I wanted to do was sit down
I might be a stranger but that's no reason to ignore me
Who's in the box anyway?

No harm in looking
Speechless
As I glare in astonishment at the reflection
It's the stranger!

Helen Blake (16)
Adams' Grammar School

Magic Within

Why have I been left out? I would watch them turn themselves into trees or stir fireballs towards the sun. 'You had to be born with it,' they'd say. Were all of them born with it? I remember a time when we would joke about such things, never thinking that it was true.

I always made fun of my friends if they said they believed in it. It was him who was the worst. I hate him. I hate seeing him making a lantern with his hands. I hate seeing him put a difference in the weather.

'Powers beyond belief,' they said. If it was beyond belief, why did they have it? Right now I meet a crossroads. It says, 'Follow me, I will bring you the sweet taste of revenge.' But it also says, 'Follow me, I will show you the cool security to cope with them.'

If I agreed to the first I could get back at him and all the rest who wield my want as if it were a toy. If I agreed to the second, who knows? I could become like them, I could be better than them.

What if you choose the middle of the crossroads? What if I showered their flaws on them as I stabbed at them with my own superior power? They would be pitiful, pointless pests, especially him.

But what if I was the same as them? What if my own gift was special and it just took longer? Will I destroy him and the fool at the crossroads? I suppose the real question is what if the true magic to master is the imbalance within?

Ata Kyereme Boafo (16)
Adams' Grammar School

An Artist

It comes to me in my sleep.
Sometimes I'm up all night. Mauve.
Just a dab to the left, right a bit
and down . . . colours pouring out my head while the flock
lie dreaming of motor cars
and data sheets.

Commercial. More commercial.
What do they know about it?
Awake again only this time it's clearer.
Yes . . . that's it. Canvas. Frantically
I clear some space and work

knowing full well what will happen.
Morning and I'm down the gallery avoiding the grey security guard
wrapped up in last night's football scores.
Motionless, emotionless, content in his black and white world.

Home again. Easel. I place a piece of
my soul back against the fridge.
Discarded for now but forever in my consciousness.

James Sullivan (17)
Adams' Grammar School

The Painter

The stage is set and a goal awaits.
A white void with depths of infinity
staring deep into my mind. Searching.
Focus. I say and begin my travels. I must reach

my destination if I am to banish the bleak before
me. Patience. That is my ally on my quest.
It will guard me from dwindling time
and unlucky ends.

Like magic, I reach and like a magician
I stretch out my wand. This day a sunset scene
will adorn the canvas as a portrait of my dreams.
And now I begin to paint. My brush a channel

from the far worlds from which the sunset had
come. I must be careful. I must not leave any
white of the previous sky. Patience will shield
me. My goal is a sunset success.

Kudjoe Kyereme Boafo (16)
Adams' Grammar School

Waiting

It was out of the box,
Lying in front of me.
I sat in the public toilet
To get away from it all,
The walls dark, sick yellow.

I didn't want them knowing yet.
No way. Then the questions would start.
Whose is it? When was it? You're only 17.
The truth, I didn't know the answers.

It felt like forever. Eternity.
The dingy, dark, disgusting floor
Where my test lay. Tick-tock. I
Looked at my watch. No way, five more minutes.

The siren wails, accident on the
Motorway my car radio said. Three minutes,
I don't want this child. I am not
Ready for this responsibility yet.

What if it is blue? What if
it is red? Confused. In a daze.
Both will change my life, I reckon.
One minute, getting closer. It's positive.

Edward Cratchley (16)
Adams' Grammar School

From This World

My heart skips a beat,
You would think I was in love
Wouldn't you? But I'm not.
I lie here today, the world spinning freefall
And I'm not even turning.

I see my family around me,
You would think it'd be a celebration
Wouldn't you? But it's not.
I see them looking at me, teary-eyed and looking
And I'm not even crying.

I see the earth, the sky and the sea,
You know what has happened now
Don't you? I do as well.
I have your realm and everything in it,
But I'm not even from this world.

Chris Walters (16)
Adams' Grammar School

Sonnet

Her body coated in chocolate-flavoured skin.
A heart full and true with yummy caramel.
A perfect face from her forehead to her chin.
Tall, smooth, sexy legs perfectly parallel.
She sits on her throne like a goddess,
Wrapped in clothes, which turns a man to dust.
She invites me into her room to undress.
To commit a sin such as tempting lust.
She walks in with short, swaying, pearly hair,
Her long black dress, but still full of colour.
A relief landscape is shown when she's bare.
A bed in the sky nothing could be duller.
I have so many things I could say, a list.
To relax on her silver lips we kissed.

Jon Kuiter (15)
Charlton School

Penniless Period

Just one promise on top of another
The way I'm on a leash is substandard
I've tried my hardest to have a father
But instead I've drawn out a dad
I have been locked inside his gifts for years
But when I am weak her heart is massive
He can't see me for free without seeing tears
Then they burn a hole in his love like acid
Only escape is on the tip of my tongue
How many people are self-appointed
Judges who judge, determined to get me hung
From a girlfriend noose in our penniless period
Please let me climb back into the hole
I am determined yet vulnerable.

Jamie Slater (15)
Charlton School

Love

The sun shines as I sit here alone,
Endless questions swimming in my head,
Waiting for a call on the telephone,
Want to chat of the things that were said,
Confused about my feelings for you,
Sunlight dancing on the ceiling above,
Can you phone me and give me a clue?
We need to talk to discuss our love,
Time is passing and still no sign,
Do you think I should make the first move?
Birds are whistling on the washing line,
Are you and I still in the same groove?
I dream then I hear the phone ringing
And this makes my heart feel like singing.

Charlene Worthington (15)
Charlton School

Paper Round Sonnet

Each freezing winter morning I awaken,
To the strident ringing of my alarm,
I leap out of bed, body a-shakin',
I wash my face, dress, suddenly I'm calm.

I slurp a cuppa, eat some dried-out toast,
Then out I go, into the wintry cold,
Get on my bike, I love pedalling most,
Collect the papers and each one I fold

And put them in my bag to keep them clean,
I rush to deliver the daily news,
Up to the houses I'm creeping unseen,
I try to be hush but I've squeaky shoes.

My last delivery, I'm chased by a hound,
I pedal home, returning safe and sound!

Michael Venn (15)
Charlton School

My Sonnet

Now that my worst fears have been confirmed
There is a scream that is locked up inside
The images of horror, I squirm
I stare blankly into space, nowhere to hide

That night I heard something I shouldn't
A lump in my throat and a longing tear
I wanted to take it back, I couldn't
Hushed cries that kept on ringing in my ear

As I quietly waited time did not stop
Everything continued like nothing was wrong
The work, the routine, even the clock
The minutes and hours endlessly long
There is nothing left to be lost or won
The life that was once there now forever gone.

Emily Ford (15)
Charlton School

Newquay Experience

As I wander from the bursting car park,
The crash and tumble of the white waves
Carry through the air like a great white shark.
The number of surf hostels have saved
The local surf scene from being extinct,
The sand and stone that line the shore,
The surfers waiting for that perfect wave
On the brink of stardom and looking for that supreme board,
Surf schoolers look out of place in blue wetsuits,
Run down to the sea in a long snake line,
When the tourists ignore the flags and loot,
The locals can't stand the crowds and climb
Back up the hill to the calling coffee shop,
I have been both people, so stop!

Richard Atherden (15)
Charlton School

The Last Goodbye

Why does it happen to everyone?
It's such a deeply distressing time
Why does it happen to your special someone?
Everyone tries to act all happy and fine
But it's hard when I'm feeling all the pain
All I need is my special someone back again
I have to think what will she gain?
No more pain, the worst thing is having to pack
I just want things to be back how they were before
We had many good times together
Remember all the time I spent with her
Those memories will stay with me forever
Just remember she loved me very much
But if only I could have just one more touch.

Rachel Evans (15)
Charlton School

Space

As I look up at night the sky is bare,
There's darkness, a wisp of cloud and the moon.
For hours on end I could look up and stare
At the bright stars, hung in the massive room.
Like time it goes on, it will never end,
Stars in the sky, with nothing around.
Yet from those jewels in the sky, we all descend,
Each part of our body from toe to crown.
Billions of planets out there alone,
Without the tiniest life to its name.
Gas giants or rocks, soft or solid as stone.
None in our system are nearly the same.
    And is there life out there? We do not know.
    Not yet anyway, until we can go.

Lee Dickenson (15)
Charlton School

Gone

You went away and left us on that day,
Not even a phone call to say goodbye,
There were so many words I couldn't say
Every time I asked for you, they would lie
They'd say I couldn't see you anymore
And that you're living in a better place
Even with all the pain that I endure
I would give anything to see your face
Every day I think of you, where you are
Wondering if you're still thinking of us
Sitting all alone, waiting in your car
Coming to see us right now, just because
You miss us just as much as we miss you
And I want you back right now, we all do.

Emma Woods (15)
Charlton School

Beauty Dead But Unforgotten

Staring into her oceanic eyes,
He realises her beauty is so true,
Her outward adornment was not a lie,
Her soul each day was born again, brand new,
Beauty of hers was innocent, so pure,
Some people have only one half a heart,
A life of pain that is hard to endure,
His beautiful girlfriend a work of art,
Now leaving her casket deep in the ground,
One single red rose to stand for their love,
Lay sorrowfully there aside the mound,
As he walked away the sound of a dove,
The unfading beauty of a quiet soul,
There she lay the dead quiet heart still whole.

Catherine Stone (15)
Charlton School

Ocean Blue

I sit and look at this beautiful pier
With memories and images flooding me,
Images of brave soldiers who died out here
There is emptiness as far as I can see,
It is for the sailor of our fine England
Blue of endless beauty stretched before his eyes,
As he leaves his safe home by shore and by sand
The strong and final vision before he dies,
How can this have such wondrous destructive power?
Such an elegant element of this land,
As waves come roaring past they grow like towers
This evil force that Mother Nature should ban,
Taking away the dark and leaving the fair
A fit grave for the sailors, the men who lie there.

Rhiannon Jones (15)
Charlton School

A Wave

All life is like a continuous wave
It starts with a ripple and ends with a clash
It wears down the rocks to form a dark cave
When it grows bigger and makes a huge crash
Also it's calm and flows very softly
It's peaceful and quiet and all you can hear
Is the tranquil wave flowing along slowly
As if the sea was shedding one giant tear
When a person grows older they build in strength
Gaining knowledge and wisdom during their life
It rolls over and collapses, the end of its strife
The wave ends its journey on a beach of sand
Like death leaves nothing in the palm of your hand.

Jackie Downing (15)
Charlton School

Sonnet

As I sit in my room thinking of life,
Yet again I hear the distant crying,
I look out the window and see the strife,
I cannot believe the pain of dying,
It's hard to believe of someone going,
When no one you know has ever gone,
Why do they go if only knowing
That loved ones grieve willing one another on?
After a while the crying ceases,
But still the pain is there just hidden away,
I look again they are all in pieces,
No tears here just people wanting to stay,
I sit down again and think of it all,
I don't feel myself, I'm starting to fall.

Amanda Long (15)
Charlton School

Time

As time flies by with the birds and the breeze
Happy faces, as they don't know their fate
The smile and glee as they wander with ease
But no one yet knows, they'll just have to wait
The seconds tick by through minutes and hours
Until that day comes when we are no more
There'll be no more left, the time devoured
Nobody knows when they shall close that door
When darkness will come and the light will go
And there'll be no change between day and night
But until that day comes we will not know
How we'll go, if we'll be able to fight
In the end we will find, when that day comes
What waits for us when our time is all gone.

Sarah Dyke (15)
Charlton School

World Cup Japan/South Korea 2002

It kicked off with Senegal beating France,
Sweden first for England, Mills messes up,
Eight for Germany, the Saudis no chance,
Argies fall to England, now it's our luck,
Portugal and France are not having fun,
Japan and Korea are loving it,
England are held to 0-0, not much passion,
Not very good for France as they exit,
Denmark are thrashed, it's looking up for us,
Ireland goes out, penalty shame for them,
The three Rs crush England's hopes with no fuss,
Korea shock Spain, the goal not a gem,
Brazil and Germany win, the hosts fall,
Ron wins the cup but he can't keep the ball.

Glyn Hughes (15)
Charlton School

Ellie

One Tuesday after I came home from school,
I was thirsty and so I had a drink.
In the garden, my dog played with a ball
And she was running too much and didn't think to stop,
She passed out on the grass in a heap,
I ran outside to see what happened,
I thought that she had fallen asleep,
I went to her and her collar I slackened.
She was breathing but her eyes were shut tight,
My mum came running to Ellie and me,
When she saw, she knew something wasn't right,
As Ellie was waking up and could see,
We took her to the vet's to be checked up
And when she returned, she acted like a pup.

Michael Woodward (15)
Charlton School

Space

Eternal darkness, all sliding about
Empty space, stacked full of nothing at all
Tiny little lights that will never go out
A streaking flame and a blazing fireball

But what lies beyond, that can't yet be seen?
Behind the darkness and beyond the light
A giant planet, with a moon that gleams
Huge clouds of water vapour, what a sight

Then beneath the clouds a world of life
Vast oceans, very wide and very deep
Space is silent, but the world is so loud
Never silent, the world can never sleep

For man has changed it, for good or for bad
There is no going back, so don't be sad.

Chris Read (15)
Charlton School

The Match

Trying to play sport on a rainy day
Takes time and energy for you to play
The goalkeepers diving into the hay
Cold weather's going in the month of May
On the pitch I'm looking to make a pass
Can't see anyone, so I go on my own
It's half-time and we head back to class
If I do not play well, I will go home
Back on the pitch to face the second half
The crowd are cheering, we start to play well
I am starting to feel a pain in my calf
My calf is burning like the heat from Hell
The pain is getting to me, I limp off
All I see above me is a black moth.

Michael Ellis (15)
Charlton School

Gone In 60 Seconds

Cars are what we want, cars are what we get
How many times have I twisted the wheel?
10 cars, be mine today, before sunset
The dusty road slides past under my heel
The lines of the colour and the shiny paint
0 to 60, I feel the need for speed
The more I looked, the more I felt faint
Police cars, I don't pay them any heed
Pressing the brake because I see the curve
Creatures standing locked in my headlight
Turned the wheel, missing the turn, so I swerve
All sharing one moment of pure fright
Sitting in its garage, its paint all dusty
The tenth car is so old, its wheels are rusty.

Paul Briscoe (15)
Charlton School

Fishing Trip

Down to the fishing pond we went at three,
rod and reel and my sandwich box too.
I chose my normal spot next to a tree,
as I tackled up, I heard a cow moo.
With my rod set up, I cast the bait in.
Sitting on my chair, I opened a tin
of bait for the hook and up came a fin.
Down went the float and into a fast spin
and across the water the line did take,
causing my rod to bend over double.
Deeper the fish went, down under the lake.
It went for the weed, asking for trouble.
I pulled and pulled, like I was in a war.
It was the biggest I ever saw.

Michael Robinson (15)
Charlton School

The Prison

With its gentle and friendly appearance
And its caring and cerebral tutors
In the weekdays it takes a prison's stance
With its cruel staff and broken computers
But only in the pupil's innocent eyes
To the parents its completely different
They cannot see through its clever guise
To them it is full of kind sentiment
I wonder to myself why it is so
When we get punished for eating our food
We get an unkind penalty I know
Our judges do not believe it is so rude
When we are thrown in our prison cells
Where we wait for the concluding bells.

Steven Robinson (15)
Charlton School

I Will Sleep Better

They write songs about it,
They write poems about it,
They even run up phone bills about it,

But how come I sleep better without it?

Love is hard
And something I really don't understand,
Do we actually know when it's right to say . . .
'I love you'?

I suppose it is one of those things,
Which could even be left to chance,
Or fate I suppose . . .
I'm not quite sure . . . really!

Although I am sure of one thing,
That I fall in love too easily,
I need the support
And the comforting arms
Of another.

But I will still sleep better without it
And I will live better without it,
Although I will always want it.

Kerry Williams (16)
Charlton School

Untitled

If I were a colour, I'd be blue
Because I would be the deep blue sea

If I were an animal, I'd be a cheetah
Because I'd be faster than lightning

If I were a flower, I'd be a rose
Because I'd smell just as nice as you.

Kirsty Carless (12)
Madeley Court School

Feelings

Winter came upon me,
Like a ton of bricks,
Snow fell down as I walked
Into the empty streets.

I was shaking and shivering,
My cheeks wet and cold,
I felt empty and alone,
Because I was all on my own.

My feet went left, right, left, right,
Following each other one by one,
My heart beating violently,
Under my soft face.

I was shaking and shivering,
My cheeks wet and cold,
I felt empty and alone,
Because I was all on my own.

Stephanie Easthope (11)
Madeley Court School

The Reader Of This Poem

(Based on 'The Writer of this Poem' by Roger McGough)

The reader of this poem
Is as blind as a bat
And as helpless as a rat
But the reader of this poem is also
As thick as a tree
But maybe as green as a pea
Is as strong as a wire
Gosh, I wouldn't want to get caught in a fire!
Is as smelly as a skunk
And as stupid as a punk
He/She probably chokes on Coke
But I sure hope the reader of this poem
Sure knows how to take a joke.

Tina Chick (12)
Madeley Court School

What Are You?

I am the colour blue
because I am cool

If I was an animal, I would be a cat
because they're sweet

If I was a place, I would be the beach
with the splashing waves

If I was a book, I would be 'Girls In Love'
because Jacqueline Wilson is my favourite author

If I was a school, I would be Madeley Court
because it is great

If I was a famous person, I would be Christina Aguilera
because she is groovy

If I was a teacher, I would be Miss Stafford
because she is kind

If I was a season, I would be summer
because it is sunny and bright.

Jemma Keefe (11)
Madeley Court School

The Pretty Flower

There was a flower that was bright and red,
It was ever so sleepy, it always wanted to go to bed.
The flower was as big as a tree,
It always liked to dip in the sea.
The flower had sharp, spiky leaves,
But they always ended up small like bees.
The flower was very pretty,
It was ever so gritty.
There was a bee that annoyed the flower,
So it went so mad it struck up loads of power.

Tina Harris (11)
Madeley Court School

An Australian Trip

I wander around Australia,
I see some wonderful sights,
There's a bridge called Sydney Harbour,
It looks lovely with its lights.

Then there's Ayres Rock,
It's a big red hill,
In thousands of years,
It will be there still.

The Great Barrier Reef
Is a sight to behold,
There are a lot of different fish,
Or so I've been told.

I see lots of wildlife,
Koalas, wombats and kangaroos,
The way things are going,
We'll only see them in zoos.

I wander around Australia,
There's lots of sights to see,
I hope it doesn't get spoilt,
For you or for me.

Ashley Burrage (11)
Madeley Court School

If I Was . . .

If I was a colour, I'd be purple
Because it is royal

If I was an animal, I would be a mouse
Because they are small

If I was a place, I would be the sky
Because I could see everyone.

Suzy Gibb (11)
Madeley Court School

My Dream

I hear a tap, tap, tap at the window
there's a man looking in

I feel a draught on my feet
he's blowing at me

I hear him whispering in my ear

I turn to look at him
but he's gone and I don't know where

I am really worried, I feel cold sweat
run down my neck

I see a shadow getting bigger and bigger

I feel something dripping on my face
something cold, something wet

I rub my eyes and open them
and everything is back to normal

What a relief, everything is back to normal.

Sioney Steventon (11)
Madeley Court School

Australian Life

I go inside the Australian bush
And hear crickets rubbing their legs.

I go inside the Australian bush
And see snakes hanging from trees.

I go inside the Australian bush
And feel the smooth leaves from the trees.

I go inside the Australian bush
And taste the rain from the wet season.

I go inside the Australian bush
And smell the fresh trees and plants.

Alan Burrage (11)
Madeley Court School

Why?

Why do the birds sing in trees?
Why do the leaves follow the breeze?
Why do the horses eat the grass?
Why do people call girls 'lass'?
Why does the sun go up and down?
Why is chocolate always brown?
Why do girls wear high heels?
Why do big brothers always make deals?
Why do trains go really fast?
Why do people study the past?
Why do boys crop their hair?
Why is a girl donkey called a mare?
Why are children really loud?
Why are parents really proud?
Why do people always lend?
Why is this poem coming to an end?

Jordan Fox (11)
Madeley Court School

Colours Everywhere

I am blue, as bright as the sky
I am brown, just like a pie
I am red as blood
Just like Red Riding Hood
And a little silver just like my gun
A little black just like night
A little orange, oh too bright!
A little green just like grass
A little pink, oh I gasp
A little white, as white as snow
A little purple, oh my toe
That is all the colours I know!

Zara Tomkinson (12)
Madeley Court School

Imagine You're A . . .

Imagine you're a monkey,
swinging from tree to tree.
Imagine you're an ant,
as big as me.
Imagine you're an owl,
teaching in a school.
Imagine you're a dog,
guarding a pool.
Imagine you're a mosquito,
dancing in the gym.
Imagine you're a snake,
as small as a pin.
Imagine you're a shark,
doing ballet.
Imagine you're a human,
up the top of a mountain so far away.

Talia Ellis-Jeffries (11)
Madeley Court School

If I Was . . .

If I was a colour, I would be red because I am hot!

If I was an animal, I would be a fish
Because I could swim to the bottom of the ocean
And lie on the seabed.

If I was a place, I would be the sky
Because I am light and beautiful.

If I was a car, I would be a Subaru,
I would be fast and furious!

If I was a book, I would be a romance story
Because they are wonderful!

Holly Spiers (11)
Madeley Court School

My Pets

I love my pets,
I love to watch their every steps,
My kitten pounces,
My dog lounges,
My bird cheeps,
My gecko sleeps,
What more pets do I have?
Well, I play with my cat,
While my guinea pig taps.
What else do my pets get up to?
While my friendly girl dogs play in the park,
The buster boy dogs mark,
What do the cats get up to?
Tigger prowls through the grass,
Molly tries to comb her fur although it is a great big mess!
My kitten is evil,
Oh what a sad story this is,
One morning when my kitten was on his murder spree,
He didn't even notice me,
As I gazed out of the window,
I saw the murder take place.
The bird fell down with beautiful grace.
My pets get up to many things!
My kitten is a murderer,
Sheba is a sleeper,
But I still love them
And that is a story about my pets!

Samantha Lister (11)
Madeley Court School

What Am I?

I have big brown eyes and very happy ears
What am I?

I am black, brown, white, ginger and grey
What am I?

I have a long coat and very white teeth
What am I?

I have a red collar and a beard
What am I?

I have a black button nose and it is always wet
What am I?

I have four legs and a tail
What am I?

Lewis Davia (11)
Madeley Court School

Home Is . . .

Home is the warm depth, rising through all tingly.
Home is a sculpture, full of love and thought.
Home is a soft fur rug you lie on near a hot flame fire.
Home is a blanket to warm you up at night.
Home for me is in Britain.

Home is full of laughter,
Home is full of memories,
Home is full of personality
And home is full of joy,
Home for me is in Britain.

Home is what you make it,
Home is where you take it,
Home is where you can share aspirations,
With family and friends,
Home for me is in Britain.

Danielle Evans (12)
Phoenix School

Save Britain

Wet weather, cold and grim,
Cities grey, smoky and dim,
Slowly, surely pollution fills the air,
But no one thinks or bothers to care.

Take a trip to the end of land,
See the fine yellow sand,
The blue shining ocean deep,
Isn't this something we should try to keep?

Walk along the high hilltops,
Look down at the steep steady drops,
See the tiny dotted sheep,
Isn't this something we should try and keep?

Into the forest where the sun can't shine,
Aging oaks from the start of time,
See the innocent animals sleep,
Isn't this something we should try and keep?

Into the swamp if you dare,
Watch out for an ogre there,
Quickly, quietly up it creeps,
Isn't this something we should try and keep?

Environment first is what I choose,
Britain, I never want to lose,
These ancient lands, folk and law,
Is what I want to keep for evermore.

Lyndsey Pitchford (12)
Phoenix School

Fruit For Days

British fruit is ripe and juicy, sweet and red on ripe,
Different colours for different months
And tastes for different days,
The British fruit grows nice and large,
That's British fruit growing in a tree, red and ripe.

Katie Jennings (11)
Phoenix School

Britain - A Place To Call Home

A cloud of grey smoke erupts from a city,
A city where people are living,
This heavy population is down to us Brits,
In the country that we call Great Britain.

A drop of drizzle is a heavy shower,
The sun, almost always is missing,
Behind all this darkness, our life is not bad,
Because this is our homeland of Britain.

The smoke clears quickly, the rain fades away,
The clean countryside, mostly hidden,
An area, fresh with life and clean air,
A green home, we *proudly* call Britain.

The united hearts of a small island is,
A sign of the love for our kingdom,
A kingdom as great as its neighbours in the world,
Our United Kingdom of Britain.

A friendly life, filled with happiness,
This wonderful place is well known,
A wonderful place, a heavenly place,
Britain, a place to call home.

Scott Peters (12)
Phoenix School

Britain

B ritain is busy with people here and there, Britain has people almost everywhere,
R uled by the Queen means Britain is best, it is certainly better than all the rest.
I mportant Tony Blair has taken us to war, living in Britain is definitely not a bore.
T owns and cities are all around, litter is all over the ground,
A ll the shops are always full, full, full,
I mportant, powerful Britain isn't dull, dull, dull!
N o, you won't be snoring because Britain isn't boring!

Emma Childs (12)
Phoenix School

Telford Kids

I see people playing,
Smelling air in the park,
Tasting the wind on their tongues,
They touch the softness of the air,
Hearing cars zooming by,
Children crying,
Parents sighing,
The local football match is in full swing,
Boys are kicking,
Injuries from rough running,
Mud splashes as bodies crash,
The air has an autumn smell,
They touch the softness of the chilly sky,
Running and jumping without care,
The day passed smoothly by,
In the park, kids are both rough and nice,
Hearing different sounds from far away,
Rain or shine, it's always a happy day,
The smell of fresh wet soil,
Branches snap and break,
Leaves crunch underfoot,
Living in Telford is really neat.

Sasha Crossley (12)
Phoenix School

Britain Is Great

Britain is cool
Cold winter, not anymore
Food is nice
People are cool
People do not ignore
Summer and autumn have just begun
In summer people have water fights
Violence is not here anymore
Just games and fun.

Nathan Harris
Phoenix School

Britain

Britain, Britain, the good old English fry up,
With your British bulldog who's only a pup.

Britain, Britain, the lovely Sunday dinner,
But you will have to worry because it won't make you thinner.

Britain, Britain is very bright,
Everywhere you look it seems right.

Britain, Britain, the big Union Jack,
You go for a picnic in the countryside with your backpack.

Britain, Britain, go out to watch the footie,
In the middle you eat a chip butty.

Britain, Britain, in the pub with a pint of lager,
With your old man, your father.

Aimee Topping (12)
Phoenix School

Complaining About Home

Home is an isle called Britain
Floating in the Atlantic

Home is where we invent games
And become brilliant at playing them badly

Home is a place where kings and queens
Rule over everything

Home is where we hate tourists
But hate it when they hate us

Home is a place where we complain about rain
But when the sun beams down we moan

Home is when in the holidays we flock to Wales
To groan about the sheep.

Grace Hickman (11)
Phoenix School

The Great War

'Come on Britain'
'Go on lads'
They'd said a million times
They treat us all like heroes
And then send us off to die

They say that we are brilliant
They say we are the best
They said that we would win
They make a plan that kills
The men and sends
The survivors back to the rats

The British, French and the Scots,
Fighting together for once
If the Germans and the Japs think they
Are gonna kill our men
They shouldn't expect such an
Easy ride, we'll fight back all the time
Even after the government lied

'Come on Britain'
'Go on lads'
They'd said a million times
They treat us all like heroes
And then send us off to die.

Mathew Growcott (13)
Phoenix School

Britain's Colours

Green is lovely, green grass out on a midday field
Yellow is the bright sun which forces people to head to the beach
Red is the poppies turning up in November
Blue is the cloudless sky which holds the tweeting birds
Pink is the tiny little flowers that pop up everywhere
Black is the pitch-black sky which upon it is the cheesy moon
These are the colours of *Britain.*

Amy Newell (12)
Phoenix School

British Animals

English dogs always lie on logs,
Irish deer have lots of fear,
A Scottish wren flies across now and again
Over the woods and down the glen,
He flies high and low in the rain and in the snow,
A Scottish rabbit runs far below bouncing in the snow,
It's a lovely sight to see them play
All through the day and into the night.

William Bradley (11)
Phoenix School

Britain

I like Britain, it's my kind of place,
I like Liverpool 'cause they're ace,
I like roasters 'cause they're lovely,
On a Sunday I like a bit of bubbly.

I like Britain, you can see it in my face,
I like Britain 'cause I've built a base,
I like Sunday 'cause of its lunch,
I like boxing 'cause you get to punch.

Brett Shaw (13)
Phoenix School

Britain

Britain is the best
We're better than the rest
Don't fret to ask me why
I just ate apple pie
Eating our Sunday lunch
We look like a right bunch
This is our sense of humour
It's not a dirty rumour.

Natalie Edwards (13)
Phoenix School

Britain's Great

I wake up to a golden morning,
Minty fresh and green,
The wild hills and all to be seen.
The squeak of a bird holding up its wings,
Watching as it sings.

The busy roads and the traffic lights,
The tall shops and huge great heights.
The rain soaking me till I'm dripping wet,
Have you decided to come to Britain yet?

The clothes designer new,
Great for me and you.
The sun, bright as can be,
The shimmer on the rivers and sea.
People work hard in and out of work,
Running home from school, giving Mum a huge great smirk.

The parks tall, trees and kites,
The rosy towns and sights.
The jolly people and their kids,
I look in a shop window, there I see a dog and a kitten,
The wonderful life in Britain.

Nikita Soltys (12)
Phoenix School

Britain

Britain is a peaceful place
So please do read this at a pace
Britain is the place for posh
And where Becks spends his dosh
We always drink our cups of tea
Upon the sand and by the sea
Our weather is extremely bad
And it make us really sad
So come on everyone who lives here
And give Britain a big cheer . . . *wow!*

William Gittins (11)
Phoenix School

What Does Britain Mean To Me?

What does Britain mean to me?
Rainy days, cold, wet weather
Chocolate biscuits dipped in tea
Autumn colours, the reds and browns
Cold wind blows through your hair
Summer days hotter than ever
That's what Britain means to me.

Fields and fields of cattle and sheep
Going to watch a film at night
Roads and roads full of cars
The blues and the greens
Rows of houses in a line
I wonder which one of them is mine?
Friends playing in the street
Laughing, joking as they meet
That's what Britain means to me.

Aimèe Glover (12)
Phoenix School

British Money

It stands in piles and can be alone
No one ever has, but everyone wants to own
It gains you things but can also lose
It keeps you happy and keeps you amused
It keeps things rolling, things tickin' on
It can all be there, but it can all be gone!
It brings people joy, happiness in their lives
It can also cause fights, even guns and knives
People use and lose every single day
The British money and that's the way!

Mike Lewis (13)
Phoenix School

School

School is boring, my friends are snoring
And the rain is pouring.
Lessons are giving me depression
And the teacher is *screaming* with aggression,
The boy next to me is trying to give a good impression.
When sport was taught at our school,
I'm going to die, well that's what I thought!
English makes me peckish,
The girl behind me is being childish,
The teachers are creatures,
They're such *screechers*,
Each with distinct features,
When the teacher mentions *detention*
I get back my attention!
Ring, ring, time to go!

Emily Barratt (13)
Phoenix School

Britain Poem!

When I think of Britain,
It makes me think of home,
Down at Ketley Park I play,
Often I will roam,
When I walk on the park, I watch the boys play footy,
Sometimes I join in on the long green grass,
Usually when I'm bored
Me and my friends climb up the tree in the windy weather,
Or instead we swing on the swings,
In the cold, dull weather we all sit under the slide,
When the clouds come out we carry on playing.

Emily Smith (11)
Phoenix School

Britain

Britain is the red, white and blue,
Scotland, Wales and English crew,
We all are British and proud to be,
Because we carry a lot of history,
World War I and World War II,
Fighting for our country, that's what we do.

We won the cup in sixty-six
And we love our curries, fish and chips,
We love to go to the pubs and drink,
Till we lose control and cannot think.

Our environment can be lovely,
But sometimes can be scruffy,
With built up cities that have no green,
To beautiful countryside that is lovely and clean.

I love Britain, what more can I say?
I love it more each and every day!

Stacey Roberts (13)
Phoenix School

Great Britain

Britain is full of different cars
Other people chill out and go to the bars

Britain is full of rain
But soon it will be summer again
Summer is very bright
Then it gets dark and you turn on the light

Britain is full of fun
Better than your friends and your son
So this is what Britain is like
Goodbye for now, I'm off on my bike.

Holly Jones (13)
Phoenix School

School

Maths is good but English is the worst of the rest,
Drama is brilliant, it's the best of the rest,
We sit around and act out, it seems like you've got a hundred pounds,
Assembly is fast, catches everything up,
The teacher is snappy,
She is quick and deadly,
She will strike at any time,
So you have to be quiet or else she'll be on the telephone line,
At break time it's great, I hang around with my mates,
We go onto the field,
The grass shines like a silver shield,
I have tuck that is crisps and a drink or two,
That gets me refreshed, not like bathroom shampoo,
Dinners are revolting they smell disgusting too,
We would like something hot and wonderfully new,
Something that's better than a smelly old shoe,
Homework is tiring and hard to do,
I wish we could just flush it down the loo.

Andrew Thorpe (11)
Phoenix School

British Food

Food, food, lovely food, how I really like it,
But not peas, oh not peas, how I really hate it,
Sausages, eggs, burger, beans and potatoes,
Jelly, ice cream, chocolate bars and tomatoes,
Hot dogs, noodles, spare ribs are nice,
Sweetcorn, carrots, curry and rice,
Apples, bananas, grapes and pears,
I love honey just like bears.

Chicken, turkey, lamb, pork and beef,
I like sweets but they're bad for your teeth,
Egg mayonnaise, bacon, pizza and berries,
Cheese, ham, tuna, kiwi and cherries.

Shaun Rafferty (11)
Phoenix School

What Does Britain Mean To Me?

What does Britain mean to me?
Britain means to me, close family,
So listen up and you will see,
Just what Britain means to me!

Milky white chocolate,
Milk chocolate too!
So many places to buy it from,
Oh what will I do?

Big concerts are held here,
In the NEC,
Busted, Christina including Girls Aloud,
So many more to see!

Spring, a joy,
New, smelling flowers,
Newborn lambs,
Cool spring showers.

So now you know
Just about what Britain means to me,
So come along and really see
What Britain means to me!

Chloe Hocking
Phoenix School

Britain

B ritish hair is very funny,
R ed, pink and blue,
I t is spiky and stripy,
T wo Nike ticks or one?
A very big hairstyle or very small?
I n Britain our hair is so mad,
N either good nor bad.

Martyn Carey (11)
Phoenix School

What Britain Means To Me!

What Britain means to me,
It's just like a magic key,
With all the great
Secrets waiting to be opened by me.

When I am at home,
My family is great,
Watching TV is wicked,
EastEnders and Coronation Street
Are the ones to grab, they're fab!

British food is fab,
Chocolate biscuits,
Now they're the ones to grab,
Fish and chips are yummy,
They also fill my tummy.

When you wake on that autumn morning
And you see that spider's web gleam and shine,
You know you're in Britain,
Small Britain,
Small and crazy Britain.

This is what Britain means to me!
Now I have opened small Britain with my little key,
Now it's time for you to come and see!

Nicole Dickenson (11)
Phoenix School

Winter

W inter is on its way
I nviting snow on the way
N o hope for May
T ickling Christmas on the day
E ating Christmas chocolate away
R eturning only for Christmas Day.

Babra Yasmin (13)
Phoenix School

Britain

Britain
Britain means
Britain means to me
The shops in London, designer ones
And the food from all over the world
But most of all, I really love
When autumn comes
Picture the wind blowing
All the colourful leaves you crunch and kick
As the clock goes tick
Big Ben strikes again

All the cars we invented
My favourite is Mini and Jaguar
Only the best
And chocolate
Cadbury's chocolate
Cadbury's should have a halo
Wherever we go
We're pleased on what we have
I'm British
I'm proud

We have cities and countryside
We're bound to find a friend
A friend in the whole world of mine
Is here in Britain
Wherever we go, we're never alone
Because simply and satisfactory
Britain is my *home!*

Poppy Durnall (11)
Phoenix School

Home Sweet Home

When I step into my home,
It feels like I step into a comfortable dome,
My garden's big,
My dogs dig,
Without that nowhere's my home.

Then I start school,
I must admit it's pretty cool,
First I go to registration,
Where I see my form friends,
Then the bell goes and we're on the move,
But before you know it, it's 3 o'clock,
What shall we do?

I finish school at 3.15,
By 4.00 I am out and about,
That is what I do when I'm home,
I love my home,
It's warm and cosy
All the time.

I look forward to night-time,
I sit in front of my TV until 9.30,
Then I crawl up the stairs
And climb into my bed,
I fall to sleep,
But then it's morning again,
So then the story of home
Starts all over again.

Ben Richards (12)
Phoenix School

What Does Britain Mean To Me?

What does Britain mean to me?
The Union Jack or afternoon tea,
What does Britain mean to me?
I'll look really hard to try and see.

Autumn leaves in the park
Or twelve at night in the dark.
What does Britain mean to me?
I'll look really hard to try and see.

Or what about a Sunday lunch
Or maybe roses, a whole big bunch.
What does Britain mean to me?
I'll look really hard to see.

Or what about some pop stars
Or maybe some of the fancy cars.
What does Britain mean to me?
I've looked really hard but I cannot see!

Samantha Jones (11)
Phoenix School

My Favourite Weather

My autumn weather
I love the autumn weather
It's the build up to Santa
I sit on my window sill
Watching the glowing leaves shining at me
Shining at me as if they're smiling
They twist and turn, making a blanket on the paths
I love the autumn weather
What comes next? . . . Winter.

Becky Jacques (11)
Phoenix School

Britain

Britain's never hot or never cold,
You whine when you're young,
You moan when you're old,
You're sick of your wife, you take the car,
To flirt with the chicks at the local bar,
Your husband's a slob with a bottle of beer,
You get stuck with the ironing to clear,
Beer and drugs,
Teenage thugs,
Your eldest is clubbing, you say, 'Not too late!'
She comes in the next morning at quarter to eight,
That is Britain, gum, litter and rain,
But anywhere else would not be the same.

Kristy Williams (12)
Phoenix School

Your Home

Your home is not just a place,
At home you feel safe,
At home you feel relaxed,
At home you have friends.

Your home is not just a house,
At home you feel comfortable,
At home is your family,
At home you are loved.

Your home is a special place,
Your home is your surroundings,
Your home is your belongings,
Your home is your home.

Samantha Woods (12)
Phoenix School

I Love My Home

I love my home and all it holds,
It's full of memories, happy and sad,
I have a place that is all my own,
It's where I feel safe even when I am alone.

I love it in the summer,
When the garden is full of bloom,
I watch my bunny running around
And listen to all the summer sounds.

I love my home at Christmas time,
When it is full of beautiful smells,
It is cosy and warm,
It is the best place to be,
It is the place I like to be with my family.

I love my home because it is where I belong,
It is where I have great times
And where I feel I am never alone,
It is special and warm because it is
My home.

Adele Godsil (12)
Phoenix School

Oh The Beauty Of Great Britain

I look around and I see fields, green as the trees,
Fresh as the air, within the countryside,
I see a patch and there something lies,
A scrumptious pear, oh the beauty of Great Britain.
As the sun shines bright,
Cows, rabbits and oak trees are in sight.
I see the post box gleaming red,
Post is put in with stamps of the Queen's head,
Every one in different colours but mainly gold,
So as I've said and as I'm told . . .
Oh the beauty of Great Britain!

Jessica Hayward (12)
Phoenix School

Bonfire Night

As the sun shines down on all,
Sadly rain decides to fall.
We all watch the fireworks,
Ever so bright,
They lighten up the night.

Roars of laughter and excitement,
As the dark sky becomes alight.
The fairground's full,
Nowhere is ever going to be dull,
On this special Bonfire Night.

Bangs, whistles and more
Add to the atmosphere,
Like a speeding car,
No one going very far,
Gathering around the fire,
Whilst the flame gets higher.

More gather around, lights flashing,
Bottles smashing,
All is loud on this very special
Bonfire Night!

Kirsty Hutchinson (14)
Phoenix School

Britain

B rilliant summer sun shining bright,
R ainy spring, cool at night,
I cy winter - stay inside,
T umbling autumn leaves a-glide,
A lways so unpredictable,
I n Britain we never know,
N ever know what our day will bring.

Emma Jamieson (12)
Phoenix School

My House

My house is made of all kinds of bricks
Not all of the stringy little sticks
It has wonderful pieces of furniture
Our glass case scorpion is cute and miniature
I live with three of my family
And we all get along very happily
We have a great computer
We research some great things like Jupiter
Our house is full of African pictures
But when the lights turn off, they look like witches
We have red and yellow walls
They don't go with all of my footballs
At the back we have a conservatory
Up and downstairs we have a lavatory
At the end is the garden
When it comes to summer it begins to harden.

Jonathan Leonard (11)
Phoenix School

Britain

Home is fish and chips on a Friday,
Home is the rain in the summer,
Home is a place where we all vote Labour, then wish we hadn't,
Home is a place where we wish it was sunny then complain
that it's too hot,
Home is a place where road rage is king,
Home is a place where we watch everything America does,
then copy them,
Home is a place where the father is at the pub and the wife is
stuck with the kids,
Home is the graffiti that lines the roads,
Home is our kingdom and ours alone.

Rachel Smith (12)
Phoenix School

October Wind

October wind is very cold
And very bitter too.
People make cups of tea to warm them up,
But after they need the loo!

The cold wind blows through long hair
And makes us feel alive,
But when the temperature's below freezing,
We like to stay inside.

When it snows it is freezing
And you might have a very bad cold,
Then you'd have to stay inside
And have loads of tissues, loads.

Jodie Shepherd (11)
Phoenix School

Britain

Britain is a popular place to live in,
Places to go, people to see,
The people of Britain care and understand other nations,
Their cultures, beliefs are taken into consideration.

The town centre in Telford,
Is a place where you could spend hours shopping,
The park makes fun come to life for children and adults alike.

Altogether Britain is a big group of friendly people,
We look out for each other, help people get better,
Raise money for others,
Britain is great!

Samantha Mathars (11)
Phoenix School

Britain's Birthday

Hip, hip, hooray
It's Britain's birthday
With the drunken dogs
And the football hooligans
People running down the street
Mums screaming at the kids
Hip, hip, hooray
Police on the beat
Burglars with their smelly feet
Dogs relieving themselves
No one to pick it up
Hip, hip, hooray
Mad mums driving to school
Children shouting, 'I don't like school'
Have a peaceful day
Hip, hip, hooray, it's Britain's birthday.

Will Sherwood (13)
Phoenix School

Neighbours

I like the people across the road
They have a pond and lots of toads
My neighbours are so very cool
We always play in the swimming pool
They have a big garden and a big home
With so much to do, there's no time to moan
We have parties all year round
Lots of music to make your head pound
I like my neighbours they're so cool
If I moved, I'd be a fool!

William Baxter (12)
Phoenix School

A Sinister Story

The mortar shell takes flight
People stare into no-man's-land with spite
Soldiers pray for respite
Countries' flags float like a lonely kite

Gas shells hit the ground
No one hears their deadly sound
Panic! Gas masks to be found
Many men make one side outstand

Men stare in disbelief
As a lone tree sheds its last leaf
While in the mission brief
Soldiers prepare for certain grief

Life in war is not all glory
It is like a sinister story.

Liam Jarvis (13)
Phoenix School

What Does Britain Mean To Me?

What does Britain mean to me?
A hot coal fire and a cup of tea,
The farms and all the countryside
And the funfairs with all the wicked rides!
I love it when the sun is shining
And I have picnics outside instead of being inside dining,
When it's raining the flowers grow,
But the bad weather scares away birds like a scarecrow,
Our country is like a busy bee,
So this is what Britain means to me . . .

Carolanne Hill (12)
Phoenix School

What Does Britain Mean To Me?

What does Britain mean to me?
A windy day by the sea,
Fish and chips wrapped in paper,
Harry Ramsden's the one to cater.

What does Britain mean to me?
Big Ben stands up tall for all to see.
Mini Coopers, Jaguar,
With one of them you could go far!

What does Britain mean to me?
Lots of soaps for all to see.
Coronation Street, EastEnders
And all the Premiership's defenders.

What does Britain mean to me?
A lot, it's where I live you see.
Britain is my country,
Britain means a lot to me.

Kirstie Pritchard (11)
Phoenix School

Britain In The War

Winston Churchill the jolly fat man
Led his troops into little Japan,
The rain stopped pouring,
The Japanese stopped snoring,
The royals went into hiding,
The troops in their tanks went riding.
Rivers in Japan started to flood,
People in hospital lost all their blood.
Winston gets the word,
He drops the bomb,
Boom! Japan has gone!

Tom Rowberry (11)
Phoenix School

Britain

What does Britain mean to me?
Rain maybe?
Mini Coopers and Jaguars
Or a road of cars made of tar.

Looking up at white fluffy clouds,
While lying in the sun.
Sunday roasts and a stroll in the park,
The smell of petrol all day long.

Playing football and all kinds of sport,
Watching films at midnight,
Fish and chips,
Chocolate is yummy and it fills my tummy.

Cold winter nights and hot summer days,
Watching TV with your feet up and relaxed,

This is what Britain means to me!

Chris Lumbard (11)
Phoenix School

Britain

Being British means to me:
A spot of afternoon tea under the great oak tree,
Picking berries down a country lane,
Putting them in a pie and eating them like you're insane,
On a Sunday have a roast,
Hitch up your caravan and away to the coast,
Most people come to see the castles and the old sites,
Going up north to see the glamorous Blackpool lights,
Go see a footie match or world-class kick-boxing fights,
Have walks down a warm yet breezy summer night,
A dip in the sea, bone-chilling I see.

Johnathan Lloyd (13)
Phoenix School

Britain

Britain, Britain is a dream,
Never dirty always clean.

Baking in the evening sun,
In front of the fire with a hot cross bun.

Playing in the paddling pool,
Dress a snowman like a fool.

Raking up the silver leaves,
Rolling up your cardie sleeves.

Raining, raining from the sky,
But do not worry, please don't cry.

Cos summer's almost here again,
So shut your moaning and don't be a pain!

Nesha Aslam (12)
Phoenix School

Homework

The tree blows,
The leaves fall,
The squirrels run,
The children call.

Fast they run,
Fast they fall,
Cut knees,
Kids standing tall.

Bike rides,
Walks in the park,
Fairs opening,
Dogs as they bark.

Rebecca Parry (11)
Phoenix School

A Soldier's Life

How does a soldier live?
Does he ever sleep?
How does a soldier live?
Can they smell the dead men?

How does a soldier eat?
Does he starve or does he feast?
How does a soldier eat?
Do they use a knife and fork?

How does a soldier die?
Does he die a painful death?
How does a soldier die?
I don't know
But Britain lives on to fight the war.

Simon Akerman (13)
Phoenix School

Life In The Trenches

Homesick, cold, lonely, wet,
Starving and scared,
We're pessimistic
And frightened,
We're learning about war;
It's bloodshed and ill wounded,
We're learning about the fatigue and suffering,
We have no hope; dampened spirits,
We stumble as the bombs fall
And run for our lives,
The limbs of men fly through the air;
Replacing birds in flight.

Alex Green (13)
Phoenix School

School

School is boring when the rain is pouring
I've got to keep awake or I'll start snoring
First impressions are important in lessons
Or the teachers will show their rising aggressions
Teachers are strange creatures
With horrible features
They give you detentions for not paying attention
Or acting like you're in another dimension
Oh no, the bell's gone, time for food!
By the way, it always looks like someone's spewed
Friends, friends, what could you do without friends?
Always making amends
The bell's gone - home time
Now I can truly relax my mind!

Sophie Davies (13)
Phoenix School

British Schools

British schools are such a bore,
You just wish you could walk out of the door.

You arrive to your lesson as late as can be
And you quote the line, 'She isn't giving a detention to me.'

Best thing about school is all the sport,
Probably because it doesn't need much thought.

All the teachers look like creatures,
Especially all their nose hair.

But when you're there, you just don't care,
Because it all becomes a blur!

Alasdair Jarvis (13)
Phoenix School

Schools In Britain

School is so boring,
All my mates are snoring.

The teacher keeps on shouting
And I'm going to give 'em a clouting.

Now I've got a detention,
But I'm not going to cause attention

And perhaps she will forget,
But I'm now starting to regret

What I did,
It was a bit stupid.

All my mates will go home
And I will be here alone.

Christopher Horler
Phoenix School

Britain Is A Funny Place

England is a funny place,
Lots of disputes and fighting.
England is a funny place,
Lots of glory and knighting.
Ireland is a jolly place,
Booze is always on the mind.
Ireland is a jolly place,
Always a leprechaun to find.
Scotland is a chilly place,
Sticks and stones are thrown.
Scotland is a chilly place,
'I can't see Nessie,' they moan.
Britain is a funny place!

James Ellis (13)
Phoenix School

School

School is always boring
Each day with different lessons
Some days the rain is pouring
Making everyone have depression

Teachers are creatures
Who teach cocky kids
Each with distinct features
Making people flip their lids

One lesson left
As time goes by slowly
Putting my brain to the test
Saved by the bell eventually.

Linsay Donegan
Phoenix School

Typical English School Day

Most people say school's boring,
It almost always sends you snoring,
Lessons send you into depression!
The food makes you feel nude,
Home time's the best bit of the day,
That's the time to commit the crime,
You always get detention,
We wish to be in another dimension,
Friends always make amends,
School's boring,
It sends you snoring.

Samantha Jacques (13)
Phoenix School

Britain

What does Britain mean to me?
The lovely colours of the autumn leaves,
The weather, cold and I am deceived,
Also the double-decker guided tours,
The Union Jack and the Queen, the laws,
There is no law against me in my drumming shed.

What does Britain mean to me?
It means the rugby, the morning dew
Playing out and people telling on you
Saveloys, chips and them chicken dips
Fields, countryside, the birds and a bee
Britain means everything to *me.*

Oliver Pickering (12)
Phoenix School

What Does Britain Mean To Me?

What does Britain mean to me?
It means the winter days
With snow and frost
Covering the ground oh so soft
Christmas time, have presents and toys
Making snowballs and hitting the boys

The cinemas and ice rink
Where we watch and skate
On the freezing ice with your mate
Telford's ground where they win and lose
And the dads go home and drink some booze.

Jake Luckman (13)
Phoenix School

Britain

Wet summer days by the seaside,
Or picnics in the garden.
Not a greater place have I spied,
Than our merry old Britain!
Off to the chippy, Friday nights,
Or lovely roasts on Sundays.
On windy days flying a kite,
These are the old Britons' ways.
Now we're crackers for a curry,
Maybe even a Chinese,
Our old ways changed in such a hurry . . .
And one more thing if you please,
Cos now we're not just British,
We're Japanese, Asian,
We're South African and Polish,
American and so on!
I thought I might just mention,
That Britain has really changed!

Emma Roker (14)
Phoenix School

My Neighbours

I am glad I have good neighbours
We always have a party
They always give me presents
They are very considerate
My neighbours are the best.

Their house is always neat
And always well presented
They have got massive hearts
They are so, so quiet
My neighbours are the best.

Shane Gleave (12)
Phoenix School

Britain

Cream tea and delicious sponge cake,
Scones with jam spread generously,
Apple pie freshly baked
And a fine china set containing steaming hot tea.
That's what Britain means to me.

The sun arises with a warm glow,
The birds singing in the quiet breeze,
Light shining on terrace houses all in a row,
Awakening the town, the skies and the trees.
That's what Britain means to me.

Buckingham Palace surrounded by guards,
Protecting the Queen and her pearls,
Everyone has a place for her in their hearts
And she has a place for Britain in hers.
That's what Britain means to me.

The 60s - they were fantastic,
Or so our parents say,
Mini skirts, platforms and groovy music,
People partying every day.
That's what Britain means to me.

The British accent and the stiff upper lip,
Putting your pinky when you drink, in the air,
Don't gulp down your drink, but sip,
It's our right to say what's decent and fair.
That's what Britain means to me.

Shakespeare, the man with words,
The playwright and poet,
Remembered by generations for years,
For his famous plays and occasional sonnet.
That's what Britain means to me.

Heidi Soltys (13)
Phoenix School

What Britain Means To Me

What Britain means to me,
Digestives dunked in my tea,
Going shopping for boots and clothes
And also the lovely smell of a rose,
Football's OK I suppose . . .

If I saw a flying pig, then I would stare,
I'd never ever eat a pear,
In the winter there is lots of ice
And in the summer it's really nice,
I also enjoy my rice.

Big Ben is a very big clock in London
And it is so lovely when the sun goes down,
If this poem is driving you round the bend,
Then you will be relieved that it is the end!

Erika Peake (11)
Phoenix School

What Does Britain Mean To Me?

What does Britain mean to me?
The crispy sparkling leaves on the trees,
They deceive me thinking they are fresh poppadoms,
The gorgeous chicken tikka masala, *yum, yum!*
The digestives, I eat them as fast as I can, licking the choc,
The whizzing fast double-decker buses, *wow!*

What does Britain mean to me?
Football stadiums coloured in where teams lose or win,
The Telford ice rink, *weeee!* It's scary.
The Union Jack is our flag, we should be proud of it.
When Big Ben strikes *ding-dong!*
Fantastic TV soaps including EastEnders!
Britain means everything to me!

Ahmed Hussain (12)
Phoenix School

What Does Britain Mean To Me?

What does Britain mean to me?
Britain means the Union Jack,
Lovely autumn colours like red and orange,
The good old Queen at Buckingham Palace
And whilst you are down there
Look at Big Ben if you get the chance,
Lots of money and pennies,
That is what Britain means to me.

What does Britain mean to me?
Rainy days and bad weather,
Chocolate digestives in your cup of tea,
It soon will be sunny,
TV soaps, EastEnders and Coronation Street,
Fields and countryside, both have the same rotten smell,
That is what Britain means to me.

Dean Barnes (12)
Phoenix School

What Britain Means To Me

What Britain means to me,
A little island around a big sea,
The smell of England, the smell of summer,
People growing old but not getting dumber,
My mates, the weather, the smell of fresh leather.

My cat mint cars,
Curries and Indians,
Chocolate dreams
And cold ice creams.

Laughing and joking,
People not poking,
That is what England means to me!

Chris Hull (11)
Phoenix School

The Good Things About Britain

I like Britain because it has the game of football,
Watching the ball bend into the top corner of the goal.
I like Britain because it has fish and chips,
A great meal to have on a Friday night.
I like Britain because it has huge shops,
You can buy anything, from clothes to food.
I like Britain because it has the Mini, a car that has a British heart,
It may be small but it has an attitude.

Jonathan Farley (12)
Phoenix School

Winter

W ater frozen, not a drop to drink, everything turned to an ice rink
I n the snow we play all day, making snowmen in a funny way
N oses cold and freezing feet, fingers numb, oh what a treat
T rees are bare, not a leaf to see
E veryone moaning, can't wait for spring
R oasted turkey in the oven, it's wonderful, it's Christmas
but it will soon be spring.

Jade Fiddler (12)
Phoenix School

Britain

I live in the British Isles,
Its beautiful countryside, which runs on for miles,
Its seas are blue
And the sky is too,
The mountains and rivers are ours to view,
There's no better place
That I'd rather be,
Than here in good old Blighty.

Stuart Job (13)
Phoenix School

The Missing Things In Life . . .

The yell of a mighty blow,
The ol' giant fountain of blood,
Everything covered in snow
And seeping through the mud
Planes flying overhead,
Making a lot of noise,
Dropping bombs making a deathbed,
No peace and no poise,
Why oh why did I ever join?
I miss my family, even the dog,
They don't even pay me a coin!
To fight and kill and swim through a bog!
If I could wish just one wish,
I'd wish to be home with a beer, oh I wish!

Rebecca Beddow (13)
Phoenix School

My Dog, Molly

I have a dog called Molly,
She is always very jolly,
She greets me with her wagging tail,
Sometimes even brings the mail!

Her coat is black and shiny,
Her ears as soft as silk,
She jumps and leaps
And runs around,
Her feet don't even touch the ground!

I love my dog, Molly
Because she's my best friend,
She's always there to listen,
On her I can depend.

Jodie Thomas (11)
Phoenix School

What Britain Means To Me

Britain means to me,
A nice warm cup of tea,
Relaxing in front of the TV,
Britain means to me.

Britain makes me think of,
Being able to go out and shop,
Going on the streets and seeing a cop,
Britain makes me think of.

When I think of Britain
And all the things I've written,
It really makes me realise,
What Britain means to me.

Harriet Blower (11)
Phoenix School

Britain Means To Me

Britain means going to school,
Britain means going to be cool,
Britain means staying up late,
Britain means hungry, saying I ate.

Britain means playing with my friends,
Britain means reading my book,
Britain means doing my homework,
Britain means making new friends.

Britain means going shopping,
Britain means doing my work,
Britain means watching TV,
Britain means moving from one school to another.

Natasha Griffin (11)
Phoenix School

What Does Britain Mean To Me?

What does Britain mean to me?
All the British actors from Coronation Street,
All the British boy bands that no one can beat
A lovely evening in the car round the country
And the food and drink from all over

Britain means to me
All the different wildlife and animals
And all the different quiz shows on TV
But most of all the different sports
Like rugby and football

All the different book writers
And all the different singers
That is what Britain means to me.

Rebecca Maiden-Jones (11)
Phoenix School

Dark Times

It was cold and breezy
And I felt miserable and wheezy,
As I walked deeper,
The hill seemed steeper,
I slipped to the ground,
With a big *bound!*
Down I fell,
Tumble,
Rumble,
I gave a groan
And had a moan,
Help!

Annabelle Heath (11)
Shrewsbury High School

The Finite Always

O! Where has he gone?
Y'know . . . that bothered boy,
Who needed me . . . always.
I just can't seem to find the guy who left at 7.05
And 'ran' home, high on the adrenaline
That I used to supply him with . . . always.
Maybe he's lost in timekeeping, always checking the clock,
Two minutes after the last time,
Leaving time for a timeless goodbye of overrated metaphors,
Which would have been spent saying nothing,
Yet meaning more . . . always.
Even the coffee shop has packed up so as not to remind us
of hours spent
Deep in each other's person. Happy to wait for that one stolen kiss,
Leaving a well of desire in each other's hearts . . . always.
I searched in the park; crept back to our patch of green wavy grass,
Where we would lie as one, making shapes out of water
floating up high
And you told me stories and we screamed, laughed, *loudly!*
As we were the only people there . . . always.
I'm sure the pool feels colder now I'm not chased by the boy,
Who couldn't help but canoodle, even though he knew
he'd make time,
(Enough to catch a canvas sack's worth of autumn)
To hold me longer, later . . . always.
Wistfully slide into sombre satin
And on this 180th moon of our time together,
I just can't tell if the sun will rise in the east for us both.
Yet until it does, the crumpled feathers of my eiderdown
Will prick me with sadness,
As I will feel the throb of the faded smallpox . . . always.

Harriet Davies (17)
Shrewsbury High School

At The King's Court

(A sequel to 'The Laboratory' a dramatic monologue by Robert Browning)

Wrapped in furs, with a dress of rustling silk
My hands clad in gloves that were whiter than milk,
I danced and I whirled the whole evening away
Bright and so happy and laughing and gay.

But under my dress, in a small velvet case
I carried my poison, covered up by lace,
Every so often, I touched the small phial
Waiting and watching for chance all the while.

The moment, it came quickly! Pauline, I saw
Left her wine on a table next to the door -
I struck in an instant! My fingers did pass
The phial over and poison into her glass.

I saw colour spread quickly, then sink and disperse
In my head I saw black horses, a coffin, a hearse -
And when Pauline did drink and wine stained her lip
I knew life from that favoured body would slip.

Sure enough, in an hour she fell to the ground
From her lips came a pained and torturous sound,
The company gasped, many ladies did faint
In the aura of death that the poison did taint.

Unnoticed, I slipped quickly into the night
My now empty phial hidden from sight,
I jumped into a coach, bade the driver drive fast
For I knew that my rival had lived her last!

Madeline Wright (14)
Shrewsbury High School

The Bottle

Out comes the cork and all at once,
Like a dark coat
You swamp me.
Breathe in,
Thoughts of you; potent. Breathe -
Out. Sighs
Of empty and forgotten worlds.
If I could frame you;
Square outline for a fighting phantom
Twenty twirling, turning memories . . .
- I saved it
A tiny bottle full of shells
- A souvenir
Of that turquoise day where the sand
Prickled and itched on our skin, the sand worms
Under our toes, trails,
Passing patterns, I knew then
Movement, change
- It wouldn't be far.
    Reflections
We smiled at each other, later we ran
Jumping on our shadows as they grew longer
Chasing the light
And the distant shapes, I held on tight to that bottle
Then I knew
I wouldn't drop it.

Heidi Browne (17)
Shrewsbury High School

Alone

The sinister atmosphere surrounded her,
She felt the cold breeze flowing against her red cheeks,
Quietly whispering at her,
She hugged her coat around her
And pulled down her woolly hat.
The night lingered a still numbness.
She felt it building up, layer by layer,
But, she just stood there, all alone, in an unbearable darkness.
She roamed the craggy, steep valleys,
Wandering around like a lost sheep.
Suddenly,
A great sheet of lightning spat over the valley,
She stood there, shivering with fright,
The storm was electric,
It was silent and sudden,
After each crack the darkness would reappear,
The only light she had was the flashes of lightning,
When it went off it illuminated the valley.
It was a stunning sight.
She had a rotten lean-to for shelter,
But, she lay there,
Sound asleep she went,
Her tension faded away,
Her elusive sense of fear crept out of her
And was filled with an eagerness to find her destination.

Sarah Lee (12)
Shrewsbury High School

Spooked

Her body found floating down the cold river
Her grey eyes glazed, her face pure white.
The wind gives a moan, the trees all shiver,
The atmosphere's tense, a feeling of fright.

Blood trickles away into the dark murky water,
From the hole in her head, a perfect sphere,
Where the bullet hit her, though no one has sought her
And no one was there to sense all the fear.

The moonlight shines down on the black misty water,
Silence is reigning the crystal clear night,
At the scene of the crime everything seems to wither,
Nothing likes to see such an awful black sight.

She shouldn't have argued or tried to fight back,
He mauled her and bruised her and killed her with one shot,
Then tied her up and stuffed her in a big sack
And threw her in the river and left her to rot.

Her body found floating down the cold river,
Her grey eyes glazed, her face pure white,
The wind gives a moan, the trees all shiver,
The atmosphere's tense, a feeling of fright.

Emma Finlinson (11)
Shrewsbury High School

Volcano

All was still and quiet,
Children playing, babies laughing,
Suddenly a big roaring sound,
Coming from the volcano,
People froze in silence,
Pets in shock.

There was a colossal bomb blast,
The volcano erupted,
It blew lava to the sky,
The sky turned a gruesome death blood-red,
Lava and rocks came down from the sky,
It was like a blizzard,
There was screaming, crying, tears.

It was all still,
The volcano had finished erupting,
It was all quiet,
Everything was covered by lava and rock,
There was nothing left,
Except a deadly hissing sound,
Left from the volcano.

Mathew Beamond (12)
The Wakeman School

My Dear Old Friends

My best friend, Russell
Who I've known for ages,
He writes stories
That are pages and pages.

My best friend, Danny
He's one of a kind,
We pinch and punch him
But he doesn't mind!

My best friend, Michael
He's big and strong,
In athletics well
He can jump rather long

And last but not least
It's my old gang from school,
Shane, Matt, Jamie and Nay,
Who are all really cool.

Matthew Pugh (12)
The Wakeman School

What I Thought Of Albert

I really liked Blackpool Zoo,
I was quite happy in my cage,
But I wasn't left alone,
So I ate a little boy who was ten years of age.
He could see I was asleep,
Resting in the sun,
But he had to interfere,
As he thought it would be fun.
His parents weren't too amused,
That I ate their little boy,
But he really shouldn't think,
That I'm a great big toy!

Timothy Carter (12)
The Wakeman School

Air

Standing in the queue, it's a scary wait.
My brain ponders my adventurous fate.
Few minutes left, the ride doesn't make a sound.
It's our turn next, my courage can't be found . . .

Trapped in the coaster. No way out.
No one will even hear me shout.
The engine starts. The car makes a move,
My courage is the only thing I can prove.
Going uphill, climbing to the top.
I know there's going to be a big drop.
Falling down at the speed of light,
Screaming to myself, *hold on tight!*
Coming out of falling, flying high.
One second I see the ground, next I see the sky.
Staring up above, the wind in my hair.
As the end comes to a roller coaster, the one that they call . . .

Air . . .

Mica Daly-Smith (12)
The Wakeman School

This Is A Poem Of Myself

(Based on 'The Writer Of This Poem' by Roger McGough)

I am the writer of this poem
I am as tall as a giraffe
And I skip down the pathways

I am as happy as the sun
My eyes are blue like the sea
My skin is as smooth as a lollipop
I move as quick as you can lick

I sleep as soundly as a baby
The writer of this poem
Is as gorgeous as can be
Never ceases to amaze
You just wait and see.

Amanda Wilson (13)
The Wakeman School

Jaguar

Prowling in the jungle green,
A little lemur I have seen,
So silently I crawl,
In the grass so tall,
I crouch and take a little glance,
At that monkey dance and prance,
I take a little jump and *pounce!*
But he's away in one bounce,
Through the trees he swings and slides,
On the ground I pound with pride,
He climbs up to the biggest tree,
But he won't get away from me,
I dig my claws in the bark so brown,
Up towards the canopy crown,
He stands before me and with a swipe of my paw,
He gets away but his tail is no more!

Katherine Hannaford (12)
The Wakeman School

My Dog

My dog's clever,
Much smarter than the rest,
But when it comes to homework,
He never is the best.

I've taught him how to sit
And also how to play dead,
But when it comes to football,
He has no clue in his head.

I've taught my dog to go north
And taught him east and west,
But when it comes to eating,
He always makes a mess.

James Travis (12)
The Wakeman School

The Writer Of This Poem

(Based on 'The Writer Of This Poem' by Roger McGough)

The writer of this poem
Is bigger than a bush,
Got a sense of humour
And is always in a rush.

As vain as David Beckham,
As sharp as a stick,
As strong as a bulldozer,
As clever as a tick.

As smooth as a bowling alley,
As quick as a fly,
As messy as a pig,
As delicious as pie.

The writer of this poem
Has a personality to amaze,
Just one in a billion
(Or so the poem says.)

Thomas Peevor (12)
The Wakeman School

Sock! Smelly!

I found my sock beneath the bed,
'Where have you been all week?' I said.
'Hiding away,' the sock replied,
'Another day on your foot I would have died.'

Danniella Shaw (12)
The Wakeman School

Cats

The feline predator teases its prey,
Hunting and killing every day.
Pinning the carpet with its sharp pointy claws,
Catching birds with its deadly paws.

She's soft in the house,
Gentle and kind,
Stands by her master,
Tall and fine.

But then when she's out,
Out of the door,
Then you'd better watch her,
Watch for her claw.

She'll pounce,
She'll kill,
Till she's had her fill,
Then she'll go back to the house,
Oh, watch out mouse!

Lynne Davies (12)
The Wakeman School

Ice Skating

This is the fun that we all think is great
Skating along with my best mate
We're off, we're going, we're going round fast
Getting faster, faster
Slow down quick, hope that's the last
Get up, don't fall
Skating away, 'Hurry up,' she calls
She's got up, she's getting closer
Spinning like a fairy
Fluttering up and down
Going round and round
We're dizzy, we're falling
Bang! 'Help!' we're calling
It's cold on the floor
My hands need gloves
It's time to get off
Slowly we're walking
To the edge of the rink
We're off and are going home.

Natasha David (12)
The Wakeman School

The Writer Of This Poem

(Based on 'The Writer Of This Poem' by Roger McGough)

The writer of this poem
Is taller than a willow
Has hair like gold
Is as cuddly as a pillow

As cheeky as a monkey
As cute as a kitten
As chatty as a parrot
As warm as a mitten

As sweet as sugar
As pretty as a rose
As friendly as a dolphin
As soft as my nose

The writer of this poem
Is so great in many ways
She's got many special qualities
(Or so the poem says!)

Katie McKay (12)
The Wakeman School

The Writer Of This Poem

(Based on 'The Writer Of This Poem' by Roger McGough)

The writer of this poem
Is as keen as a cleaner
As fast as a cheetah
As strong as a boxer

As clever as a tomato
As rich as a millionaire
As big as a door
As sly as a fox

As clean as a whistle
As sharp as a pin
As smooth as a road
As tricky as a nib

The writer of this poem
Is as quiet as a mouse
As bright as a light bulb
(Or so the poem says!)

Scott Cartwright (11)
The Wakeman School

A Monkey's Tale

I swing around the trees
Eating nuts and fruit
And start to play in the leaves
When a hunter begins to shoot

I flee for my life
And raise the alarm
I run for my home
In the middle of a farm

I reach my home
I'm safe and sound
But when I look for my son
He's nowhere to be found

I have a horrible thought
In my head
Then I shout out loud
'My son is dead!'

Andrew Steinert (13)
The Wakeman School

Silent Stalker

Deep in the savannah at the speed of light,
The jaguar kills with one instant bite,
Prowling around,
Crawling on the ground,
Desperate to stay out of sight.

The hungry cat spies its prey,
It has to eat to live another day,
It crouches down with such great stealth,
You wouldn't know it's in perfect health.

The jaguar strikes, the chase is on,
Little gazelle will be long gone,
Despite his effort he can't last,
The hungry savage is just too fast.

The jaguar's deed is finally done,
Fresh red flesh under the blazing sun.
Deep in the savannah at the speed of light,
The jaguar kills with one instant bite.

Andrew Fletcher (12)
The Wakeman School

The Big Game

An empty stadium,
The sun is rising,
Six hours till the match begins.
No noise, no sound,
As quiet as a
Feather hitting the ground.

It's 2 o'clock,
The fans arrive,
Colourful, bright, roaring people,
The players run out from the tunnel,
Intense cheer from the crowd!
The whole stadium is aloud.
Without further ado,
Let the match begin.

The Blues at home, the Gunners away,
Ten minutes into the game,
Cudicini rolls it to Le Saux,
Le Saux chips it to Zola,
Zola volleys the ball
Into the back of the net.
The crowd leap up, the roof is lifted,
Oh aren't these Chelsea players so very gifted.

The whistle is blown,
The match is ended.
A mixture of emotions fly through the stadium.
The ground is emptying,
As fast as a sink.
The groundsmen clear up,
Ready for the next big game.
All that's left is Zola's fame.

Luke Pritchard (12)
The Wakeman School

The River

Clear, crystal raindrops falling gently from the sky,
Like tears dripping down a child's face,
Making ripples in the water.

The tiny trickle travelling through
Mountains, fields and bridges too.
Towering trees, blowing in the breeze,
While the little river meanders at ease.
Then her journey comes to the mountains,
Hitting the rocks, making little fountains,
When she gets to the top . . . there's a big, big drop
And the torrent comes cascading down.
Whooshing, gushing, crashing and smashing,
No longer a tiny trickle but a fierce and mighty river.
Tumbling and thrashing, fighting over rocks,
Filling the air with a patch of white mist,
A cloud of spurting spray.
The silent valleys are no more,
But a thunderous, deafening roar!
She's rushing so fast that she's bursting her banks
And nothing can stop her now.

She's past the fast and furious rapids,
Uprooted trees and hedges, washed away river banks,
For her force is immense.
She's getting to the bottom, flowing at an unbelievable speed
And plummets into the lake below.

Finally the journey's over, no bounds,
Just a wide open space, free to roam, but sadly not for long.

As the journey's gone by, the once tiny trickle
Has changed, grown older, gone,
Lost in an ocean of drops.

Lucy Price (12)
The Wakeman School

School

The empty halls, the silent staffrooms,
Not a peep from the line of classrooms,
The echoing staircases winding up the school,
No one is there to break the rules.
But then the front door opens and teacher walks inside,
With her heavy shoes, she takes big strides,
She walks to her classroom, there she waits
For the stampede of children pouring into the school gates.
She waits.
Then suddenly the doors burst open,
Bashing, hammering, thrashing, thudding,
Thundering of feet,
It dies down as they rush to their classrooms.
At last it is lunch,
Eating, devouring, chomping through their food!
The mess is complete,
There is so much, there is nowhere to put your feet!
At last the day is nearly through,
English, French and the maths too,
The bell rings, everyone waits to be excused from the lesson,
The odd couple stay behind,
To watch detention slips fly!
The last children walk out of the school,
The cleaners clean the mess they left,
Then they return home too.
The only sound you can hear is a scratching of a pencil,
Teachers marking, ticks and crosses.
Then once again there is silence,
The winding staircases winding up the school.
No one is there to break the *rules!*

Amy Thomas (12)
The Wakeman School

The King And Michael Piers

Once up on a time, in a faraway town,
There lived an old king with a wonderful crown,
Everyone admired his golden hat,
With diamonds, rubies, this and that,
Then one day when he was sitting on his throne,
No one was there, he was all alone,
A cheeky monkey ran right up
And hit him hard with a silver cup!
As he was blinking back the tears,
His arch enemy, Michael Piers
Walked into the room with a humongous frown,
Went up to him and snatched his crown!
Said, 'You won't need this anymore!'
And threw it down upon the floor,
'Ha, ha, ha!' he cackled high,
'And now my lad, you shall die!'
At that moment, through the door
Strode the terrible Fearless Four,
'Oh help me, help me, save me please!'
The poor old king was on his knees!
'Of course your Highness, we'll do what we can
To get rid of this mean, unwanted man.'
So swords in hands, they strode about,
Piers was scared, without a doubt,
'I'm sorry, I'm sorry, now I shall go'
And he limped through the door, head hung low.
Well that is the end of my story, but
If you visit the prisons, you're sure to tut
At the old, old man, sitting in his cell,
Ready and waiting to go to Hell.

Rebecca Barlow (12)
The Wakeman School

The Rushing Rapids Of The River

The rushing starts at a mountain;
Slow as a tractor,
But soon getting quicker,
Quickly down -
As she passes meadows and fields,
Louder and louder she rushes on.

At the rapids she whirls and twirls,
Smashing and bashing the sides of the bank.
The sound is extremely loud,
The current is strong,
But she holds on.

She finally reaches the plain,
The sound gets softer, the current slows down.
She carries on to the estuary,
Hearing the waves in the distance calling to her.
A last sudden rush,
Slipping softly,
Silently,
Into the sea.

Sam Jones (12)
The Wakeman School

Kingfisher Wharf

In the garden by the slow-moving Severn,
Summer dew deep on the long grass lawn,
And the fungi on the low-cropped tree are pink in morning light
And the steps to the water are bushed with plants
As the birds start their early morning song,
And the kingfisher sits on the old plum tree,
And the fox lies down in his faraway den,
And snaps his teeth at a sleepy bee.
And the sound of the weir is clear in the morning air,
And the spider is busy in his dew-spangled web,
And the caterpillar crawls under the gate,
And it's sun-high midday heat time,
And the animals retreat into the shade,
And the thorn-sharp yellow rosebush blossoms
And the kingfisher on his proud high perch
Are the only ones who watch the river flow,
And the steps to the river are bushed with plants,
And the fungi on the low-cropped tree are white in daylight,
Summer dew has dried on the long grass lawn
In the garden by the slow-moving Severn.

Francesca Fletcher (12)
The Wakeman School

The Writer Of This Poem

(Based on 'The Writer Of This Poem' by Roger McGough)

The writer of this poem,
Sleeps like a cat,
Runs like a jaguar,
Talks like a parrot,
As nifty as a gnat!

As sharp as can be,
As tall as the BFG,
As clever as a calculator,
As quick as a wink,
As pretty as can be!

As busy as a bee,
Swims like a whale,
As sly as a fox,
As fun as a ball,
As quick as a flash of a tail!

As wicked as can be,
As cool as ice,
Never ceases to amaze,
She's one in a million,
Or so the poem says!

Kassey Mound-Evans (12)
The Wakeman School

The Writer Of This Poem

(Based on 'The Writer Of This Poem' by Roger McGough)

The writer of this poem
Is smaller than a mouse,
As keen as the River Severn
And has a friend bigger than a house.

As bright as the gleaming sun,
On a dawn fresh day,
Has a memory of an elephant
And as much as a dog to say.

As smooth as newly polished wood,
As quick as a pounce,
As sharp as a sword,
As jerky as a flounce.

As strong as a weight lifter,
As tricky as a test,
As handy as a hammer,
As assumptive as a guess.

'The writer of this poem
Never ceases to amaze,
She's one in a million billion,
(Or so her poem says.)'

Camilla Powell (12)
The Wakeman School

The Battle

The spearmen stood side by side
Their iron mail clinking
Their sandals tied
Their sharpened sticks could pierce skin
At fifteen paces with heads of tin
The army stood silent
As if time was still
Their eyes scouting
For the beasts they would kill
Suddenly a rumble came from the sand
The war was starting across the land
Then the Minotaurs came into sight
Their nose rings shining in the sunlight
The creatures' axes held high
Zeus looking down from the sky
The armies met under his cloud
He sent a fog to act as a shroud
The mist confused but it didn't last
The armies struck with a blast
There came a howl from the dead and dying
The sand turned red where the corpses were lying
The last man stood where the arrows had darted
What was this war and how had it started?
The terms had just been misunderstood
To try and make peace a brotherhood.

Bradley Edwards (12)
The Wakeman School

A Cricket Ball

A cricket ball
Starts off very small
In the bowler's hands
She does lots of things
Rolling, turning, moving
Finally it is spinning
Going down the pitch
Now it is not small
But very tall
And then it is released
Thundering down the pitch 90 miles an hour
What a power
The batsman swings
What a shot
The ball flew over mid on
But now it is reaching
The end of its journey
Finally it crosses the boundary
What a six!

Lee Williams (12)
The Wakeman School

Fear

Fear is cold and jet-black,
It tastes like lumps of sour and bitter coal,
It looks like a bottomless pit,
It sounds like someone breathing down your neck,
It feels frozen and sends shivers down your spine.

Harundeep Sandhu (11)
Thomas Telford School

A Martian Sends A Postcard Home

They feed it up and heat it,
Pull out their guts and eat them.

There are no survivors; it just keeps on sucking,
Nothing is left untouched.

It's some sort of communication system; it talks to them,
You can press a different number and a different person appears.

It tortures them by screaming a long string of words,
But they scream back and mock it.

Their paws fly across the buttons, they cry in despair,
Like they have died.

The inhabitants look at those beautiful pictures,
They look almost realistic.

It patters down like gunshots, wet and miserable,
It comes from their god above.

Rhiannon Newman (12)
Thomas Telford School

A Blade Of Grass

You are a blade of grass
You stand tall
But sometimes you go green
With envy

You get trampled on
But grow back strong
You blow in the wind
You are a blade of grass

You stand tall
Go green with envy
Get trampled on
You are strong
A blade of grass.

Charlotte Banks (13)
Thomas Telford School

Spring!

The tiny seed grows and grows underneath the ground,
Hiding under deep thick layers where it can't be found.
As it grows bigger it eventually sees light
And if you look close a little bud is in sight!

In a little more time the body will appear
And then the shape and feature will soon become clear!
There is not much movement from the little flower,
But in days and months to come it will gain all strength and power!

The seed is now a baby flower, growing day by day,
Standing small playing on a sunny day.

With the other flowers around swaying in the breeze,
Whilst standing up above are the mature oak trees,
Collecting food and water from the roots,
So then the baby flower can eventually grow tiny shoots!

Every day the flower learns something new,
Like a baby, just like me and you!

Sarah Fyfe (13)
Thomas Telford School

The Single Rose

Withering in the icy wind,
Frail and so tender.
Inviting summer long had passed,
With full bloom and full splendour.

Others still upon the ground,
Deadly misery in her soul.
Sharp silence the only sound
And still she struggles, determined.

Finally warm summer returns,
Familiar sunshine yet not the same.
Too late for the rose to recover,
Too old for this weary game.

Emma McKee (12)
Thomas Telford School

Christmas

Christmas is time of cheer,
For many on this Earth,
Bringing presents and sacks of joy,
On Jesus' time of birth.

But we always must remember those,
Who tremble all through the night,
Thinking about what tomorrow will bring,
If they will make it through the fight.

Christmas dinner is always so good,
With the family all around,
Pulling crackers and wearing party hats
And hearing the church bells sound.

No food to eat, no sprouts or meat,
As they wait for the day to go by,
No happy chatter, no strength of matter
And no more tears to cry.

So when you eat your Christmas pudding,
Spare a thought for those who wait,
For a life that won't cause so much desperation,
To be free of a world of hate.

Charlotte Nutt (13)
Thomas Telford School

Ode To A Hairbrush

Hail, o mighty hairbrush!
You make my hair simply soft.
So strong and powerful,
Absolutely wonderful!
Never shall I hate you,
Never shall i pull your spikes
Or throw you away.
Without you, hairbrush, I wouldn't be complete,
Because I couldn't be pretty or sweet!

Sophie Stephens (11)
Thomas Telford School

My Childhood Memory

The water's green, I can taste the salt,
My tension builds at the wake of the boat,
The rope goes taut, I'm huddled in a ball,
The call goes out and the engine roars.

My grip is tight, knuckles white,
The shimmer of the water is a blinding light,
My legs feel like jelly, as the power locks on,
Out of the water like a salmon's run.

Spray on the face as the wind whips round,
I'm up and alive, such an exhilarating time,
I feel a sudden rush, a beaming smile,
You just can't explain the speed and the strain.

Faster and faster across the wake,
My knees start to tremble, the body shakes,
Within a flash, my head's in a whirl,
I'm spinning around, feeling dazed and hurt.

I'm all alone, as the boat speeds ahead,
Bobbing up and down, as the skis drift away,
A shriek of delight is heard from afar,
My family and friends with arms in the air.

That beaming smile appears once again,
The proudest moment I've had in years,
You've just got to be there to live the dream,
A sensational feeling that will never leave.

Hannah Guy (13)
Thomas Telford School

Autumn

Summer has gone and autumn is here to take its place
At first the wonderful leaves of bronze, gold, green and red
Then the wind blows fiercely sending the leaves off in a race
The flowers have all gone now and the leaves are shed
The saplings are swaying; nature is saying goodbye to the sun.

Chris Flint (11)
Thomas Telford School

All Alone

I'm blue and small
And I'm all alone in this white paradise,
People come by with their trolleys,
Taking away my white dream,
Why are they mean to me, Kia from planet Kpling?

I'm invisible and nobody knows about me,
Imagine their faces if they knew,
They'd be screaming with terror and fright,
Children running, going, 'Mummy, there's a monster in the milk aisle.'
Why are they scared of me, Kia from planet Kpling?

But I wouldn't hurt them,
I may be small and blue,
With arms coming out of my head,
My skin may be rough not smooth,
Why are they nasty to me, Kia from planet Kpling?

I live in the milk aisle of a supermarket
And it may be very cold,
I know that I'm all alone
And it may not be like home on planet Kpling
But I like it here for a while, me, Kia from planet Kpling.

Jessica Halford (12)
Thomas Telford School

A Postcard To An Alien!

As the bright silvery ball reaches down to kiss the ground
and making everything light

As she tucks in her little babies into their cotton wool beds
they stand out against the silk blue blanket

Her babies also shine making little paths of light, guiding you the way,
as the blanket turns darker the silver ball gets lighter

Until the blanket starts to get light, her babies awake
and shine brightly upon a velvety black sheet.

Tanita Guthrie (12)
Thomas Telford School

There's An Alien In Your House!

I control them all,
They obey my orders;
I wait for them to sleep,
Then I show my true colours.
For what they see on the outside is just an illusion,
For my true identity is hidden beneath;
I do everything a normal parent does,
I cook their tea with hairy hands;
Then I read them a book,
With my three eyes working;
But then they're at school,
I swim in salty water, rinsing my fiery orange, scaly skin;
Then when they come home, I control them with my power,
Everything I ask of them they do;
In some ways they help me,
But they don't realise;
For they will never know,
Until that chosen day,
When I'll control the Earth!

Ben Hamilton (12)
Thomas Telford School

Bonfire Night

Bang! go the sparkling, spangly, sizzling fireworks
Against the black, moonlit sky,
Children watch in amazement as they see huge multicoloured
Spiders leap out of tiny rockets,
Crunch, crackle! goes the gigantic fire,
As its massive orange flames reach out trying to grab you,
Whoosh! go people's sparklers as they try to write their names
in thin air,

Bored adults slowly sip on white plastic cups of tea,
The fire slowly burns out,
With one last crackle it disappears.

Demi McCann (11)
Thomas Telford School

Dolphins

Have you ever wondered
What life's like under the sea?
Swimming about all day and night,
What a life it must be.

Have you ever thought
Where they all must sleep?
In their own sea houses,
With little cars that go beep beep.

I'm thinking of a mammal,
Can you guess what it is?
It has fins and a tail,
Shall I tell you what it is?

Their colour varies,
From light blue down to grey,
Yes, I am a dolphin,
Come and see me someday!

Natalie Hope (11)
Thomas Telford School

I Am A Zogo

I am a Zogo and I come from planet Nogo,
I have no bones in my M-shaped body,
Only yellow skin all over me,
My two pink plaits which stick out like antennae,
Are on either side of my big red ear,
I have three purple eyes glowing from
The top of my three long legs,
The four red noses I have are on my four feet,
Instead of my four big toes,
Two of my legs have two arms,
With one or two of my six hands each,
I am a Zogo and I come from planet Nogo
And I live inside McDonald's restaurant signs.

Rebecca Brown (12)
Thomas Telford School

Phoenix

A blessed flying incense kiln,
That burns in glorious flames,
With red scent filling the air,
An airborne volcano.

Half covered by its scorching wings,
In its bright tree, it makes its nest,
Shining phoenix, a glowing star,
Spreading ash all over the land.

A gorgeous sight, its rich pyre
Fired up with aromatic blaze!
Its scarlet eyes are fiery coals
Hypnotically fixing all.

The desert yellow wilds, the scene,
Here ends its echoing song,
With scarlet tears and mournful cries,
Mourned by the Earth, it passes away.

Yet it becomes arisen when danger looms,
With smouldering orbs of flare,
Resurrected the immortal bird on high,
An aerial incineration.

Still, it gazed upon, its combustive body,
A gliding flow of magma,
As if to its basic instinct,
Knew something was wrong.

Her charred neck held high in air,
Like a small rainbow, a symbol of peace,
But brighter glowed her plumey crown,
Singeing feathers fall to the sea.

Victor Verster (13)
Thomas Telford School

A Letter From A Martian Visiting Earth

In the private den of a human being,
There are many strange and unusual things.

They own a box-shaped item,
With many emerging arms and legs.

When people massage it, symbols appear
And sometimes bleeps and flashes when you touch it.

A tall machine rumbles and grumbles,
Because it gets pushed along the ground.

The female species torture this poor creature,
But the men never lay a finger on it.

Another creature is better treated
And gets given food and tickled.

It bleeps when it's had enough to eat,
This must be a favourite of the humans.

A hard, square screen that projects an image,
Talks and makes lots of strange sounds.

When you poke it in a certain place,
It goes silent and the picture disappears.

The next machine shows it's grateful,
When you give it a round, flat present.

If you insert the gift into its pocket,
It sings tunes to you in thanks.

A very small creature held in the hand,
Shows a moving picture on its one eye.

When you stroke the creature's markings,
The picture moves and plays music.

Rachel Lloyd (12)
Thomas Telford School

The Sunset

The sunset is a fire of passion,
Red, orange and yellow,
Often over the wavy seas.
Its colours reflect upon the clouds,
For as far as you can see.
There's a breeze blowing over the clouds,
Over the sunset's face,
If you are lucky you may see a ship or boat,
Sailing across the horizon.

Just like a blanket of red and orange,
I cannot see above the clouds,
I cannot see beneath the sea,
But I can see the sun fall.
I will always have a bright picture in my mind
Of the place where I saw the sun disappear into the sea.

Ryan Musgrave (11)
Thomas Telford School

A Martian Sends A Postcard Home

When somebody presses a button
It flashes and makes funny loud sounds.

Shows moving pictures of other people
Some people even watch themselves in there, wow!

Monster controlled by humans that sucks up
Anything that gets in its way.

Humans put things in there and this mechanical thing
Exchanges it for something that is warm and they can eat it.

A handheld flashy thingy that has moving people
And animals you can control and has lots of buttons
And makes a funny noise.

Projects pictures onto a blank screen in the middle of the world.

Edward Cooper (12)
Thomas Telford School

A Martian Sends A Postcard Home

Two boxes, one with a screen, one with buttons that are often hit,
a small long-tailed creature, that is often hit and abused.

A face with a picture of food slowly rotating, it opens up and you eat it!

A pet that rolls around on carpet with a long tail
and eats everything in its path, its tail is often stuck to the wall.

A strange face, with moving pictures, that has the power to hypnotise
anyone in its path, it makes sounds but it can always go to sleep
if you want.

A strange box that is always a different shape, it makes really terrible
sounds and is often poked or hit.

A small creature with a moving face, it is poked on a cross
and two circles.

They put them on their faces and instantly look like monsters,
with many eyes.

Patrick Lawrie (12)
Thomas Telford School

The Snail

The snail is slow and paces its life,
At a steady speed, graceful and nice.
It chuggers along like a broken printer
Or a tractor in the snow.

The snail has a mobile home,
It is a slug but with a house.
Its ugly body, just there, in our lives,
Waving its antennae around.

The snail and its silky tracks,
On the concrete, the gravel, the grass.
It leaves its calling card, its mark,
For us to discover, under the glittering sun.

Joseph Wesley (11)
Thomas Telford School

A Martian Sends A Postcard Home

They have a box that lights when given food,
It beeps and gives the food back after a while.

A creature hunts with its long nose,
Guided by a person.

It growls as it works,
Stuck to the wall by its long tail.

A box is stared at by everyone,
Showing the world.

It gives information
And carries on when interrupted.

It speaks and sings,
Playing music most of the time.

A thing is small and has a screen,
It is often attacked by a child's fingers and thumbs.

There is a thing in the sky,
That is only seen from Earth in the night.

It shines white
And changes shape.

Clare Donnelly (12)
Thomas Telford School

Gruesome Depression

Depression is dark grey,
It tastes like the rotting flesh of a tiger,
It smells like the depressing smell of a men's urinal,
Depression looks like a lengthy road with black ink filling every crack
And every gap in every house,
It sounds like the dying scream of a man,
Depression feels rough, jagged and hot.

Thomas Middleton (11)
Thomas Telford School

Being A Fish

Have you ever wondered
What it's like being a fish?
Just swimming around my bowl, minding my own business,
There's no way out,
Around and around I go, causing my own dizziness.

My golden scales glimmering in the light beside me,
My watchful eye looking out for trouble,
They named me Lee,
But what's the point in a name?

The cat, oh no!
He's coming over here,
His whiskers are twitching and he is licking his lips,
I try to look cool but I am trembling with fear.

Nowhere to go,
Nowhere to hide,
My only wish is to be in a deep blue sea with other fish
surrounding me,
I wish this all was just a terrible ride.

The cat takes a swing . . .
Phew! He missed but just by an inch,
My owners luckily come in and save me,
'Oh look Kitty, is that a finch?'
I say as a joke!

Demitria Cartwright (11)
Thomas Telford School

Autumn

Autumn, autumn, autumn
The crackling leaves, golden brown
The naked trees oh so bare
And the evenings growing oh so dark
In autumn, autumn, autumn.

Kieran Stuart Bourke (11)
Thomas Telford School

My Alien Friend

Hi, my name is Jim
I live in outer space,
I'm a weird little creature
Part of an alien race.

I have ten fingers,
I have ten toes,
They are all really helpful
For when I pick my nose.

I am really short
And my belly bulks out,
But what it is that annoys me most
Is the spout that I've got for a nose.

I can run very fast
And I can jump very high,
But now I have to go back home
To eat my tasty pie.

Richard Flint (13)
Thomas Telford School

A Man Called John

There used to be a man called John,
Everyone thought he was a bit of a con.
He bet on the horses,
At all the race courses
And he reckoned he won every one!

One day he went to a betting ring
And as usual the till went *ting.*
Though it took him a little by surprise,
To hear the horse he bet on had hurt his eyes
And he wouldn't become as rich as the king!

Sarah Moreton (11)
Thomas Telford School

Billy The Elephant

I'm Billy the elephant,
I smile with glee,
I'm Billy the elephant,
Not just plain old me.

I'm a happy elephant,
I laugh all day long,
I'm a happy elephant,
I like to sing my song.

If anybody starts to shout at me,
I turn away and laugh,
If you don't believe me,
It's even on a graph.

I'm Billy the elephant,
I always smile with glee,
I'm Billy the elephant,
So I'll never be just plain old me.

Georgina Rumble (11)
Thomas Telford School

Never Fitted In

I remember when I was at school,
They treated me like I was a fool.
Bullied me for trying to act cool,
Believe me they were cruel.

There was no fun for me,
I had maths while they had PE.
Got told the rest were better than me,
In English everybody got a 'C',
Not me, they gave me 'G',
But to that day it still hasn't affected me!

Samy Morsy (12)
Thomas Telford School

Animals

I hiss and I spit and I live in Great Britain,
I'm not quite a worm nor have legs like a kitten,
I slither around on my scaly front,
I don't squeak like a mouse nor like a pig do I grunt,
My poison is deadly if it sinks in your skin
And my fangs will leave marks where my teeth have sunk in,
I eat mice for my breakfast and mice for my tea,
They have to run wildly and scatter when they see me,
If you don't wind me up, I'll do you no harm,
But to people who do I will bite their leg or their arm,
So be nice to me because I am an adder
And if you annoy me I'll only get madder.

I run pretty fast, up to 35 miles per hour,
I pounce on my prey with such force and power,
I like to eat stag just like a lion,
I have fur not clothes, so I don't have to iron,
I'm proud of my stripes of orange and black,
Covering my front and my back,
My teeth are sharp and so are my claws,
My mane is my hair and my hands are my paws,
My name is the tiger, so don't mess with me
Or one of my brothers will have you for their tea.

Katie-Emma McAnulty (11)
Thomas Telford School

The World

The world is a lovely place
With twinkling trees and sparkling light
It's a kind and warm place
Flowers colourful and bright
That makes the days warm and wonderful
Lie down and look up at the sky
And watch the fluffy clouds go by
Sit up and watch the beautiful world go by.

Sophie Jones (11)
Thomas Telford School

Lots

Lots of things I like,
Lots of things I love,
Lots of things I hate,
Here's a taste of what I like,
A snippet of what I love
And a peek of what I hate.

Chocolate, chocolate, lots of chocolate,
Jaffotopia mad,
Orangey centre, chocolate cover,
Creamy caramel,
Soft, sticky and stringy,
Aero madness,
Chocolate bubbles,
Yum, yum, yum!

I love to lie on my bed,
Sometimes play on the PS2 instead,
I love to sit and watch the goggle box,
As my mum says,
'Are you going to sit there all day?' She nags.

I hate to get up early,
It's cold in my bedroom,
My dad sings terribly, it makes my ears ring,
My mum's so naggy, but that's part of life,
Saturday outings are so dreadful,
The supermarket we must go.

So now you know my
Likes,
Loves
And hates.

Daniel McKee (11)
Thomas Telford School

The Rattlerock

If you go down to the woods tonight,
Beware, you're in for a fright,
The animals hoot, screech and flap,
While thunder slowly claps.

Wolves howl at the moon,
Slipping out of tune,
A bear growls in his lair,
Without a single care.

Be scared if you should
Meet the beast of the wood,
With slashing claws
And a snapping jaw.

He's covered in hair,
Like a huge grizzly bear,
With glaring eyes of flame,
He's not very tame.

His huge black wings
Are to carry off kings,
His long swooping tail
Will hit without fail.

So if you meet this beast,
You could be his feast,
So be polite
Or you're gone in one bite!

The fearsome rattlerock
Is not a beast to mock,
So stay well away
Or he could come out to play!

So if you go into the woods tonight,
Beware, you're in for a fright!

Nabeel Ilyas (11)
Thomas Telford School

Who Am I?

Sitting in the corner,
Crying day and night,
People laughing and staring,
Can you imagine that sight?

No one to love, no one to care,
Only the people that stop and stare,
Now all I think to myself is,
Who am I?

I see all these families,
I think, *where is mine!*
Who am I?

No one to love, no one to care,
Only the people that stop and stare.
Now all I think to myself is,
Who am I?

Sinead O'Neill (11)
Thomas Telford School

What Am I?

I am a master at hunting,
With my perfect camouflage
And my stripy black and white coat,
My appearance is cute and fluffy,
But you don't want to get on the wrong side of me!

My teeth are long sharp fangs,
So I can eat what I want,
I eat deer, antelope and also warthogs,
When I catch them I eat them on the spot,
Then take the leftovers to my family,
Then go on the hunt again.
What am I?

Lauren Williams (12)
Thomas Telford School

What Am I?

A colossal football in the sky
A furious flame
Everlasting glow
A blazing globe
A dazzling light
An awakening alarm
As yellow as a sunflower
A colourful sunrise
A ball of fire
The colour of fresh butter
A massive lemon
A happy feeling
A bright day
The light of the world.

Emily Richardson (11)
Thomas Telford School

Rugby

Once you step out on the pitch
You feel something inside you itch
As soon as you show your mercy
You start the game and run into Percy

When you know you are really trying
It will make you feel like you're flying
When you take a nasty hit
It will make the bench a place to sit

The forwards charge with a mighty crash
In the defender's face with a frightening smash
At last the game is finally over
You forgot you weren't wearing your lucky clover.

Daniel Codling (12)
Thomas Telford School

Hockey

The swishing and swooshing of the stick,
Like the choppy sea.
The keeper of the goal is well padded
Like a wrapped-up child in winter.
The ball being hit, like an apple falling
Off a tree.
Paying for expensive sticks, like a merchant
Having gold.
The goals are high and wide, like an
Open church door.
The pitch is moist, like an autumn morning,
The teams are in the changing rooms,
Packed like a dormitory at school.
The church is talking nonsense,
Like a mad, tropical bird.
The pitch lines are like lasers,
In a fortress of prisoners.
And the teams run on, like a crowd
Of chattering monkeys.

James Turner (11)
Thomas Telford School

Shadow!

When you're walking down the streets, he is there
When lying down having forty winks, he is there
When you're climbing up huge rocky mountains, he is there
When you're on holiday relaxing in paradise, he is there
When you're having nightmares, he is there
When you're having the time of your life, he is there
When you're working hard at school, he is there
When you're playing sports, he is there
When you're upset, he is there
When you're with friends and family, he is there
Wherever you are, he is there.

Richard McGovern (11)
Thomas Telford School

The Beginning Of Spring

Spring is the rising of the morning sun, after a long and troubled night,
spring is the cavalry back-up, come to join and win the fight.
As it tears its way through the dead and springs up new life,
the animals watch as winter is gone in a swipe.

Spring is winter's downfall as it flies from its den,
creeping and sneaking to escape!
Pushing up and up till it reaches the canopy, spreading life and light
to the tips of their leaves.

It awakens the owls - the barn, tawny and brown owls
who sleep in the eaves.
Spring is a butterfly breaking free from its wintry cocoon,
pushing away from the barrier and bringing the country pleasure,
beauty and play.

Spring is when the clouds are banished and new, crisp,
fresh mornings mean the start of the sunny season for all!
So spring is the bringer of gifts in the form of flowers,
animals and birds in flight!

So spring is the end of darkness and the beginning of light.

Laura Bailey (12)
Thomas Telford School

Hallowe'en

Hallowe'en, a night to scare
To petrify
And raise your hair
Hallowe'en, a night for fun
Naughty stuff - don't tell your mum
Hallowe'en, a night for sweets
Lots of yummy, tasty treats
Hallowe'en, a night for kids
Evil pumpkins with burning lids
Hallowe'en is exciting
But beware the vampires don't do any biting!

James McIntyre (11)
Thomas Telford School

Park

The park is a temple for all us kids
It's the place we go when we close our eyelids
The screams of us all having fun
The times we jump around and run
We scream and shout and laugh
When we are all being silly and daft
The roundabout that zooms with a creak
The swing that flies with a never-ending squeak

As night-time falls the day sinks away
The kids have gone home to sleep and play
In the park, a whisper creeps around
Nothing can be heard, no screams or sound
The park is lonely with no friends
They have gone away as the day does end
The roundabout that drifts with a creak
The swing that glides with a never-ending squeak.

Louise Jordan (12)
Thomas Telford School

Football

Football, football, without you
Whatever would we do?
Such a sweet and elegant name,
It's the world's most favourite game.

There are many genius with a ball at their feet,
Like Beckham with free kicks you wouldn't beat
And Ronaldo, the Brazilian that'll always score,
Along with Kluivert that'll never seem to bore.

There are lots and lots of clubs and fans,
With the Turkish, Spanish, English and Italians,
The Italians are the ones that cheat,
The Spanish are the ones to beat.

Thomas Morgan (11)
Thomas Telford School

The Snake

The snake, he slithers, waiting for his prey.
Closer and closer, its stomach feeling tight,
He waits; he waits until he sees his chance
And pounces on his prey, causing pain and sheer fright.

A snake's smooth texture can lead you to believe,
It's warm and cuddly, just like a pet.
But if you disturb him you will soon find,
He is the deadliest creature you can get.

His tongue, long and thin, his fangs lethal
Spray venom to your eyes, blinding you for life.
The sleek and slimy snake, silently slides away,
Searching for his next victim to cause them trouble and strife.

Now his day is over, he sidles to the lake
To rest its weary body until it's time to wake.

Jamie Mackenzie (11)
Thomas Telford School

The Storm

A knock on your window
A chill down your spine,
The heart of the drums
The thumping of your heart.
Howls of the wind,
Hiding under your cover,
Golden snakes dancing,
The portal to evil.
The caging of all hope,

Nightmares come and go,
But this, this is no nightmare,
Welcome to the worst night of your life.

Hayley Downton (11)
Thomas Telford School

Whirlwind Or Me?

There's a rumble in the distance,
Is it a whirlwind - or is it me?
The noise is getting louder,
Bang!
Things are flying,
Coat here, shoes there,
Schoolbooks flung!
There's debris and litter everywhere!
Peace has been shattered!
Tidiness gone!
The noise is now fading,
Things are getting calm.
I am in the bath,
The wind has gone.

Catherine Stone (11)
Thomas Telford School

Who Am I?

I am scaly, I camouflage well.
I have a tongue like a Sellotape roll
And feet like a water balloon.
I have sharp claws with a good grip
And I eat flying creatures near the lake.
I have a tail that is quite long,
People either love or hate me.
I make a good pet,
But really, I like the heat.
They write songs about me and
I will always be a mystery to some.

I am a chameleon!

Chloë Herrick (11)
Thomas Telford School

The Sun

The sun is a blister in the sky,
The crack to a new beginning.
The sun is a sign of good things to come,
The sun is a sign of Heaven.
The sun heels wounds and hearts,
The sun can put a smile on your face.
The sun is a giant lump of warm snow,
The sun cannot be fused by all of the Earth's water.
The sun concurs dark, every day.
Can the sun really be gone? *No it can't!*
Can the sun ever die out?
The sun is a great ball of fire and
When you see the sun, it means God is happy with you.

Unnas Nadeem (11)
Thomas Telford School

Autumn

Gently floating to the ground
the leaves are red and gold.
Round, shiny conkers waiting
to be snuggled away by squirrels
preparing for hibernation.
Chestnuts to be picked for roasting.
Falling apples, damsons and juicy plums
to be made into delicious crumbles and jams.
Children preparing their costumes for Hallowe'en -
witches, ghosts and ghouls.
Then comes Bonfire Night - magnificent fireworks,
Toffee apples, parkin and cinder toffee.
Winter will soon be here.

Emma Hugh (12)
Thomas Telford School

Head Teachers

Head teachers are so strict,
They teach us not to nick.
In assembly, they pray,
And read the Bible to thee.

Head teachers are such giants,
But can be really sweet.
They teach us maths, English and science,
And about distant World War III.

Head teachers are so mean,
They plot and scheme,
They cross examine you
And dissect you.
Chew you up like a fly,
And spit you out and die.

Head teachers are not always wicked,
They give you great big stickers.
They take you on school trips
And watch the horses getting whipped,
When you go to the farm that's large,
You watch them as they make and put marmalade in jars.

Christopher Cousins (11)
Thomas Telford School

The Tiger

A tiger roams the barren land
No fertile soil, only sand
The black and orange stripes
Like a streak of light
But all of a sudden a killing is made
And soon the stripes begin to fade
Like a rainbow with all its colours, all swallowed up
But soon the tiger will have it all eaten up
The tiger is full, it now needs to rest
But the tiger knows he's had the best.

Martin Flavin (11)
Thomas Telford School

Spring

Spring is the time of year,
Where there are newborn sheep
And when the spring and winter meet
When the lambs are jumping about,
And the children, when they shout.
Oh what a lovely season it is.

With the pink blossom falling off the trees,
And the multicolours of the leaves.
With the scent of poppies and roses too.
I promise I will give one to you.
Oh the season of spring,
Is a lovely thing.

When you bite into the fruit,
When you receive loads of juice
Which makes your face screw up
Because of the sweetness inside,
It fills you with pride.
Oh what a beautiful taste!

Merrie Thomas (12)
Thomas Telford School

The Cat

The cat, creeping slowly along the fence,
The bird, quiet as a mouse.
No other sound in the garden
Except for the creaking of the wood.

The cat, hunting like a lion in the jungle,
Seizes its moment -
Feathers everywhere.
So much for being as quiet as a mouse!

Thomas Harris-Higdon (11)
Thomas Telford School

Ratty Deeds

Thirteen black cats on a wall
The bird just sang his final call
A shadow of a tree falls to the ground
Leaves blow gently round and round
A plague of silence carries through the sky
The world can say its last goodbye

Rats, rats, rats shall roam
'Til all that's left is skull and bone

Eye of frog, tail of rat
Leg of newt, ear of bat
Poisoned liver of a snake
Stir and blend, boil and bake
Kittens' claws, sap of tree
Lizard's tooth, sting of bee

Rats, rats, rats shall roam
'Til all that's left is skull and bone

Circle the cauldron, nice and slow
The potion boiling just below
A spell now is all we need
To perform this truly nasty deed
'Hokus Pokus' it's the birth
Of rats that'll overrun the Earth.

Rats, rats, rats shall roam
'Til all that's left is skull and bone.

Rachael Hayhurst (11)
Thomas Telford School

The Life Of A Sun -Haiku

An evening sunset
A golden morning sunrise
A glistening sun.

Anna Tyrpak (12)
Thomas Telford School

A Forest In Autumn

A forest in autumn is an artist's palette,
Which paints a picture on a large canvas,
Using a mixture of rich and warm colours,
Copper, brown, red, yellow, bronze and orange,
Branches are undressed and ready for bed,
Where they will sleep until springtime.
Leaves are falling down from the streaming tap,
Flooding the ground making a carpet of many colours.
The wind blows the leaves round the goldfish bowl
And they swim round and round and round
Until they finally settle on the ground.
Listen and you will hear the musical notes playing,
By the orchestra beneath my feet,
As I walk through this beautiful place in autumn.

Natalie Loftus (11)
Thomas Telford School

The Sun

Blazing beautifully, the sun
Transports the sky in its crimson coat.
It's like a red ping-pong ball
Bouncing along a blue table.
A red apple in a fruit bowl, full of blueberries,
It's like a red spot of blood on a blue sheet,
As hot as an oven, just heated up.
It's a fiery, hot furnace.
Its rays are like a lion's mane,
As destructive as a lion.
It's a rose in a pot full of blue tulips,
A red beach ball floating in the calm, blue sea.
It's the warmth that only the sun can give you.

Rickinder Chima (11)
Thomas Telford School

My Car Is A Cat

My car is a cat
A sleek, black cat.
She purrs when she is happy,
But hisses when she's not.
She has tiny black ears
Which come out at the side.
She sneaks so silently
As if there's something to hide.
Her piercing white eyes,
They light up the night.
When she sneaks up behind you
You get quite a fright.
Her racing black tyres
Are her small padding paws.
When she runs on the ground
On all types of floors.
But behold her sharp claws,
They attack you like that!
It's these very features that make her my own.
She's mine for the keeping -
For my car is a cat!

Helen Barnett (11)
Thomas Telford School

Hail Oh Polo

Hail oh Polo!
You are like a sweet
I will eat you, night and day
I could eat two hundred packs a day
You are so minty and sugar-free
I will never eat a Mars bar again
I will never eat gum again
I will never eat a Twirl again
I will never eat a KitKat again
Hail oh Polo!

Alan Thomas Watkins (12)
Thomas Telford School

The Great White Shark

Deep in the tropical seas
lives a great white shark.
Who's afraid of nothing,
come light or dark.

He's as big as a bus,
and is covered with glamorous scales.
As other fish back away
when it beats its hated whales.

His teeth tell a sign of danger,
as they sparkle, a fearsome white shine.
It carefully watches its prey
and if it sees you, then you're on a thin line!

Every time it looks at you,
it's a sign of danger,
as it watches, then kills.
Even if it's a stranger.

Each tooth is as sharp as a knife,
they can tear anything to bits.
As its gigantic mouth fills with prey,
but if there isn't any prey, then there comes a mighty fit.

All who have suffered a tragic death,
a sign is to be said,
whoever waits around,
then they may be dead.

Nathan Rooney (12)
Thomas Telford School

Skiing Haiku

Cutting through the ice
Gliding down the crusty slope,
Snow is tickling me.

Stacey Bould (11)
Thomas Telford School

The Ogre

The fearsome ogre
In all his might
Lives in a dingy cave
With minimal light

He's as strong as a lion
As bold as a knight
If you came across him
You'd sure have a fright

His warts, they bubble
All over his face
You'd never escape him
In this horrid case

His teeth are like daggers
That rip you to shreds
His deadly sharp claws
Could slice off your heads

His breath smells like sewers
As bad as his bum
Nails as black
As yellow is the sun

So if you stumble upon his cave
Such terrible things go on in there
I'd advise you to turn and run away
For you'll be trapped in the ogre's lair.

Tom Coram (11)
Thomas Telford School

My Autumn Poem

The wind has a mind of its own,
The leaves have an athlete's jump,
The trees have a sound wave's quiver
And the people have the coldness shivers.

Mitchell Hickman (12)
Thomas Telford School

Tiger Of Destruction

In a faraway, faraway hot country
Lies billions worth of gold,
But guarding it closely each day and night forever
Looms a being, as young as a baby.

Its body is strong like a great big boulder
And armoured with its thick fur,
Even the Safari stumbles
When it bites their heads off with its sharp teeth.

Its red bloody mouth tells a story of terror,
They drip with fear
As it watches its prey, day and night,
And the tiger of destruction is its name.

Its claws are sharp and pointed,
They can tear anything into shreds.
It has soft, thick fur that even daggers just bounce off
For its eyes gleam with an angry red flame.

Each claw is as fierce as each other,
Each tooth has red blood stained on it,
And anything it touches must perish,
Set by burning fiercely the tiger of destruction.

All who have stepped
On the tiger of destruction's golden cache
Remain in that hot country,
Nothing left but the bones of its prey.

Mark Cooper (12)
Thomas Telford School

Autumn

Wake up early in the morning
Stay in bed, too cold to play
Listen to the birds chirping
It's a damn wonderful day!

Ben Brierley (11)
Thomas Telford School

All Endangered Species

Panda, panda, living free
walking through the woods,
crunching on the leaves.

Panda, panda, eating your bamboo.
That's all you ever do,
just chew, chew, chew!

Like a great big steam roller,
you barge through the jungle,
crushing everything in sight,
with all your might.

Suddenly you hear an almighty bang
and black out as quick as that . . .

No more steam roller
barging through the jungle.
No more eating bamboo
and you won't die of hunger.

Where's your lovely thick coat which
kept you warm in the winter?
It has probably been bought to use
as somebody's rug on their cold, dank floor.
Panda!

Eloise Morris (11)
Thomas Telford School

Autumn Poem

Autumn prowled in the grass,
Pouncing on anything that would come to pass.
Autumn is as fragile as crunching leaves,
Yet autumn is as strong as the tall oak trees.
When autumn fades and ebbs away
We all know he will come another day.

Erin Davies (11)
Thomas Telford School

Memories

A sign saying *Nursery School,*
I'm helping in the class,
Looking about me is a wonderful sight,
Remembering when I was at nursery.

Small and tiny, cute expressions,
Little hands experimenting with paper,
Paints and crayons,
Grasping the first signs and sounds in their reading.

Secure and safe, everyone innocent and in their wonderment,
Looking forward to play time with my friends.

Sitting at that small table in my late years,
Remembering my first experiences
And feeling happy!

Aimee Tunks (13)
Thomas Telford School

The Boy

He ran down the street as fast as he could,
He had on a jacket without a hood.
He fell on the road, flat on his face,
Only to find he'd tripped on his lace.
His mum put a plaster on his arm,
Now to keep out of harm.
Up he got and went on his way
But he had to stay in the rest of the day.
His mum said she would cook
As long as he sat quietly, and read a book.
His tea was tasty, his tea was nice.
He had chicken curry and rice.

Josh Brown (11)
Thomas Telford School

The Man With Red Eyes

The wind is blowing into my room through my open window,
Whooshing past my face and stinging my eyes.
Something is in the air.

I look out of my bedroom window and I see him standing,
Standing on the edge of the cliff we call Death Point.
Something is in the air.

Suddenly he turns and stares at me with blood-red eyes,
Making me jump out of my skin.
Something is in the air.

He turns away from me and plunges into the darkness,
Of the edge of Death Point and into the fiery chasm
of the other side of life.
Now nothing is in the air.

Poppy Bennett (11)
Thomas Telford School

Butterfly

The white egg lies in the centre of a leaf,
Nothing there to do.
It waits and waits till it finally breaks,
And out comes a slimy green lava.
It ponders around, eating all the flowers
Until there is no more left.
So he decides to rest and become a chrysalis
Filling the leaf so there's no room.
After a while,
It's starting to smile
As out comes a huge butterfly.
It flies around to see the world,
To show of its lovely work.
It waits a while till it's on a leaf then lays a white egg.

Amardeep Bahia (14)
Thomas Telford School

The House

The house is a face
which gleams in the dark
its mouth is the doorway
which opens wide
to reveal the contents inside.

The eyes watch you from inside
you'd better be careful
they watch all the time
they like to watch the other people go by
as he gives a longing sigh.

His nose cannot smell
as it is all blocked up,
he needs a tissue but cannot
pick one from the box.

His hair is a dark brown
and has got no style
but a point at the top
which he wears with pride.

Charis Ward (11)
Thomas Telford School

Autumn

The orange eye in tiredness blinks
Silence as the trees prepare to stand alone, naked
Chatter of the escaping geese, talking
Crunch of the crimson, crispy leaves
As nature falls asleep once again.

Molly Clarke (11)
Thomas Telford School

The Rise And Fall

As I raise my pen into my scaly fingers
I look at the white moon with the
shiny glitter of the stars, moving through
the moon and sky.

I look at my father,
looking down where he's sitting
looking at the garden, staring at
the textured moon.

I look at the white moon,
it's gone now.
While the page and pen are lying on my desk.
I'm thinking, thinking.

David Morris (13)
Thomas Telford School

Sunny Poem

The sun is a bit like a poem,
First there is no sun
Just darkness, this is when
You have no ideas.
Then comes a little bit of light -
This is the inspiration.
Then a little bit more sun pops up,
You start to think of more ideas.
By midday the sun is high in the sky,
Your poem is now in full flow.
It then gets a little bit darker,
As the poem starts to close down.
Once the sun is down, you put
Down your pen and the poem is finished.

Laurence Tyrpak (13)
Thomas Telford School

My Poem

When I picked up my pen
I had a thought in my head
I thought, *don't leave it till later*
I'd better put it on paper.

Then came the memories of the teams
Of Manchester United
With Giggs with the run of the century
Against Arsenal.

Then with the highest transfer fee
For Jaap Stam at 10.5 million
then out he goes
Back to his foreign land.

And then we lost Beckham
To the super star team
Real Madrid in Spain.
Which left us with much pain.

Then I put down my pen
As it had turned half-past ten.

Chris Jones (14)
Thomas Telford School

Photographs

Photos, photos, pictures of ourselves,
Silly faces, happy faces, walking on the Fells.
Swimming in the pools, running in a race
Photos of the happy times, a really smiley face.

Photos on holiday, sunbathing on the sand,
Photos of my grandma, holding my hand.
Photos in Blackpool, photos in Spain,
Photos of me in the pouring rain.

Amelia Reynolds (12)
Thomas Telford School

Writing A Poem

Here I am, my pen a-poised
To write a poem about two boys
My mind, a wondering in a dream
Whilst my thoughts create the theme

The poem that I began to write
My pen flowing like a bird in flight
As the paper begins to fill
Writing this poem is quite a thrill

As my pen carries on by
My thoughts slowly begin to run dry
So now I need to ask my friend
So my poem can come to an end.

Now I leave my thoughts to rest
As I have tried my very best
As it's the end this poem I crown
Now it's time to put my pen down.

Amy Birkett (13)
Thomas Telford School

My Poem

When I got out my pen
The grandfather clock struck ten
I've had the clock since I was five
When my great grandfather died

When I look it makes me sad
When he was with me he made me glad
When he died I didn't know why
Deep inside it made me cry

If I had one wish today
I would have wished him not to die in May
An hour has gone, the clock has struck eleven
I hope to see him soon in Heaven.

Chris Moss (13)
Thomas Telford School

The Web

One idea, one thought is all it takes
To start her web off
Like a busy little spider making a home
The thought moves on

One thread, one strand gets it started
It multiplies, growing into millions of ideas
Not all can fit in; the spider decides which will stay
Most will go, those ideas are wrong for this web

One thread, one path takes it to its destination
Then so quickly like a strong gust of wind
Like a falling ranch
It's gone, the web is undone.

Marcus Atkinson (14)
Thomas Telford School

Rugby Match

I sit there watching the crowd go by
I see a glimpse of the players out of the corner of my eye.
Suddenly there's a huge roar,
Another try scored and the crowd want more,
The crowd stop roaring and it's quiet around
There's nothing, not a single sound.
The noise rises again into a cheer,
The sound of *'Swing low, sweet chariot'* is in my ear,
I join in for fun,
And soon after that, it's over and done.
Three blasts of the whistle and England have won.
I couldn't feel anything but amazed,
This was one of my favourite days.

Thomas Nixon (14)
Thomas Telford School

I Pick Up My Pen

I get ready to write as I
sit in my chair,
I pick up my pen and
run it through my hair.
I look out of the window
down at my mom,
she's standing there
chatting on the phone.
I looked around to see
what I could see,
all that was there
was the reflection of me,
I stare at my mom and
look her in the eye.
I could see my grandad it
nearly made me cry.
I still miss him deeply but
life has to carry on.
I know that I can see him
cos he's part of mom.
I get ready to write as
I sit in my chair.
I pick up my pen and run
it through my hair.

Kirsty Finch (13)
Thomas Telford School

Anger

Anger is red
It tastes of rotten mushrooms
And smells of boiled fish
Anger looks like an overflow volcano
The sound of crackling fireworks
Anger is powerful.

Louisa Piller (11)
Thomas Telford School

My Poem

I sit in my kitchen thinking what to write as
I rest my hand on the lily pads
I look into the water, looking for ideas but
all I see is the bottom of the stream then . . .

A trickle of water drops from the waterfall
I watch it as it makes ripples in the water
As my reflection slowly takes affect of the ripples
Another one drops . . .

It spreads further and further, deeper and deeper
I get more and more ideas sprouting in my head
A leaf slowly drifts into the water and sits
on top of the surfaces . . .

Drip, drop, drip, drop, drip,
The drops stop and everything goes quiet
With my hand embedded in the water as the lily pad
slowly falls into the stream,
going down, down, down!

Abi Mears (14)
Thomas Telford School

Mourning

The morning is dull and quiet,
Silence is everywhere,
The death of Charles has shocked them all,
The fun and laughter is there no more,
As the sun rises in the sky,
Mrs Jones starts to cry,
Although Charles has passed away,
The memories of him will always stay,
As the morning passes the tears fade away,
Living without him starting this day
His family will work hard to make him proud,
So he will smile down from the clouds.

Nathan Pitt (13)
Thomas Telford School

Leaves

The sun was dipping below the mountains,
She let out a weak cough,
The leaves fluttered to the ground around us,
I love the way the leaves just curl up when they have had enough,
Then they get blown away to another place,
To be at rest and are forgotten.
'Go out and be free, while you still have time,'
Were her last words to me.
I never knew quite what she meant . . . until I watched the leaves.

The seeds bloomed into flowers, which then became seeds,
'Where are you Mum?' I cried, running round the hospital.
'Bring her back.'
Nobody listened, she didn't seem dead.
How can somebody be here one minute and gone the next?

A few cubicles away, a little girl had just been born,
She too, like the leaves
Would curl up and die . . . in time.

Katie Millwaters (13)
Thomas Telford School

The Dolphin

The graceful dolphin
Is young and free
And is quite content
With his friends, in the sea.
It darts through the water
Like bird or a bee,
He sings to its friends,
Using a song that never ends.
Although this is a side to a dolphin
That you never really see,
He goes in hunting mode with a flick of his fin.
Using sonar, he finds his prey
And by taking their life -
He lives another day.

Ryan Link (11)
Thomas Telford School

Rocky Hunter

Wakes from slumber, warm yet hungry in awe of his winter coat,
still thick and glossy. Eyes alert and ready for anticipating any action,
nose like tanned leather, weathered by the blinding ball.

Walks knowingly through trees seeking frightening prey and
stands back and stretches tall on his two legs, arms above his head.
He is the tallest male of this hunting season with a taste for blood
and an evergreen heart, staring through the trees
looking at the land, as strong as an ox.

He hears a sound and crouches on all fours, breathing quickly.
He moves stealthily towards the fast-flowing spring river
and wades oblivious to the winter waters and casts his aim
amongst the depths. He is by far the cleverest fisherman of
these waters and scoops salmon upon salmon, making their
graceful yet bitter journey home.

With belly full, he peruses this fine hunting ground that as yet
still shows no sign of avid hunter or gutted carcass remains,
he is sure to keep his grounds clean and undetected.
The sound of the loon home to nest haunts his enquiring mind.

He watches above him, the bald eagle, swiftly swooping silently
over the trees like a leaf on the breeze, but even though distracted,
he is sure to keep an eye out for the threat that deters him most, the
shadow fallen over this land of his and that is man.
Whose hand-built structures are difficult to avoid and attract
this curious wonder.

For one day, this rocky hunter may end his days as the trophy himself,
displayed gaudily, as a cheap collectors' item, for all with ignorant
mind, small and materialistic to admire.

This awesome stature, this proud young grizzly bear.

Bobby Standley (11)
Thomas Telford School

Alone

A long train snakes past the horizon
All is happy, all is calm.
The Indian day comes to an end
And the gentle giants get ready to rest.

Baby elephants nestle next to their parents
They feel safe as a house.
As the leader elephant lets out a last groan
He sees this as a siren to begin his challenge.

He rustles in the bushes like a panther
Waiting for the perfect moment to pounce on his prey.
He creeps out of the bush and begins to kill
The sleeping, enormous animals.

Destroying each family one by one,
Taking a baby away from its mother.
All gone but one tiny baby.
He leaves the elephant graveyard.
The last surviving baby arises
To witness his mother taking her last breath.
All the happy memories they shared were gone
And the baby was alone.

Natalie Wood (13)
Thomas Telford School

Fear

Fear is black,
It tastes like poison.
Fear smells of smoke,
It looks like towering mountains of flame
And sounds like lions roaring.
Fear is death!

Dafydd Francis (11)
Thomas Telford School

A New Day

The sun shines through the mist of the morn
A new day is born.

The warmth and shining brightness
Comes through the sky so cloudless.

The early bird sings,
The movement of the nestlings.

Arising in their beds
The lifting of their heads

Smiling faces and cooing voices
Facing many lifelong choices.

The rosy sun shines down light
This new day is such a delight.

The new day smiles at me,
The new day fills us with glee.

A new day for all to see
I admire so proudly.

Wishing for a new day
And it's come to me today.

Siân Phillips (13)
Thomas Telford School

A Witch

A witch is coal-black
She is a frosty winter's night
In a bubbling cauldron
She is a dull, misty, rainy day
A witch is a dark, hooded cloak
A long, prickly broomstick
She is a boring television advert
A bowl of sprouts!

Joshua Wright (11)
Thomas Telford School

Mouse

Skittering, scattering
It's almost invisible,
Looks like an ant,
And smells a bit chocolatey!

Energetic like the spring,
Its tiny but big
And tastes like . . . cheese?

Short stubby legs,
For running quickly.
Plus a whip and small detector
To balance!

Covered in rags,
Black, white and grey.
Skilfully snatching snacks,
As small as an ornament, some could say,
Like a commercial against EastEnders.

Kelsie Fall (11)
Thomas Telford School

Autumn Is Here

Look up in the sky, birds migrating
Like a swarm of wasps.
Watch out on the floor, squirrels
running, collecting nuts like busy
Mums in a supermarket.
On the floor different coloured leaves
gold, red and yellow, it looks like a
carpet of rusty colours.
Somewhere on a bush, on a twig
is a spider's web with dew on it
and it looks like ice droplets,
drip-drop, drip-drop.

Hannah Remiarz (11)
Thomas Telford School

The Monster

Its eyes glare on the path ahead,
Lighting up the night sky,
It trundles along by the moaning trees,
To an area where monsters lie.

It prowls along the moonlit streets,
It roars every now and then,
It screeches at the other monsters,
Going to find its den.

When the monsters cross paths,
They screech and scream,
They lock into a fierce fight,
As if in a dream.

They lie dismantled all over the path,
Before they're cleared away.
They are not monsters after all,
They're cars that have crashed today.

Francesca Palmer (13)
Thomas Telford School

Fish

Swimming around in deep, deep water
Rocks and bridges to hide
Darting and diving
Silently moving
He swims with ease.
Searching for food
He swims to the surface
To eat his meal
And then descend again.
Round and round the tank he goes
I'm glad I'm not a goldfish!

Rebecca Cooper (11)
Thomas Telford School

The Monkey

As I swing from tree to tree, I have to think fast,
I always knew this paradise was too good to last.
Where will I go? What will I do? As I hear another almighty crash,
I always knew this paradise was too good to last.

My past life was wild, wondrous and carefree,
Things started to go wrong though,
As they took down the first enormous tree.
Now I'm constantly in hiding and fear,
Where will they go next, after they have destroyed here?

On and on through day and night,
All of the other animals have taken flight.
But I remain with fear and pain, to see what is left of my home
And not a tree is left standing, and I am all alone.

You would have thought the humans would learn,
From their other mistakes in the past.
We will rise to meet them
And make their paradise too good to last . . .

Sian Reynolds (14)
Thomas Telford School

Poem Of The Night

The sky was like a blanket of the blackest of ashes,
The stars were twinkling in the sky,
The moon was as frozen as a block of ice,
It was time to end the day, relax and block out everything.

Lying there thinking, *what will happen tomorrow?*
Thinking about the events of the day that has so quickly passed.
Staring hard into the pitch-black room like a zombie in a stare.
Slowly calming down and finally falling asleep.

Dreaming about life ending
Waking up suddenly, hearing the mumblings of the telly downstairs,
Thinking . . . *today and forever I will make the most of life.*

Anna Clarke (13)
Thomas Telford School

The Graveyard

The graveyard's million eyes stared at me as I walked up to the path,
The old house's mouth was open, begging for people to come in,
The windows were cracked and crying
As I walked up to the coffin house.

The windows of the coffin house were covered in mist,
And the door covered with net,
With spiders on.
The owl's voice said, 'Don't go in!'

The soft webs I have broken with my hand,
But brave enough, I slowly walked in.
The smell was horrendous,
This place wasn't just for humans but for animals too.

It felt like a never-ending place,
As I got trapped in,
For when I was dreaming.
The spiders sought revenge for their broken web.

I felt it was the end,
As if I too would be dead,
As these harmless creatures trapped me in
Where I would be left to die and rot.

Jasdip Koner (13)
Thomas Telford School

Stages

Seed so full of joy, innocence and potential.
Sprout growing high, reaching up to breathe.
Shoot out of the ground, it comes to admire the genders.
Leaf looking proud as it starts to resemble.
Bud - nature swelling, waiting to burst.
Flower raises its head with pride as the life is finally shown.
Death - the beauty slowly dies, withering to the roots.
Seed so full of joy, innocence and potential.

Kirstin Baker (13)
Thomas Telford School

Sunrise

I saw it start to glow,
Oranges, yellows rolled into one,
Just above the hilltop, it started to show.

Fierce with energy and colour,
About to explode,
As it grew, it became fuller.

More light as it grew quicker,
Higher up into the sky,
Like fire the colours began to flicker.

Pinks and reds began to appear,
Mixed in with the clouds,
The colours all began to smear.

An orange ball was now in full gaze,
It began sweeping across the sky,
It's beautiful, how Mother Nature has her ways.

Laura Grainger (13)
Thomas Telford School

Freedom

As he stands alone like a needle in a haystack,
Not knowing how to get there,
A small light shines as bright as the sun
And shows him the way to his freedom.

Closer, nearer
He is reaching his destination,
The light is drawing in,
Encouraging him to go on.

The light, is only a few steps further,
He shouts, 'Yes I've made it,'
Because he has reached his goal
And found his
Freedom!

Kristina Williams (13)
Thomas Telford School

Spring

Spring is a happy time for everyone
Everything new and fresh
The daffodils and snowdrops
Gather on dewy hills
The newborn lamb stands then drops

But the animals are not the only happy ones
Small children enjoy the muddy puddles
Young couples look out on spring showers
The grandparents take strolls in the park

Then Easter comes, the symbol of a new beginning
Children gaze at colourful Easter eggs
The church is filled with flowers of all kinds
As everyone celebrates together
Giving thanks for what they have got

Now this season's almost over
We are all sad to see it go
But the weather is better now
Long gone is the snow

Summer is just around the corner
Blue skies soon to come
But I can't help but miss
Spring and its frosty morning sun

Carys Greenwood (13)
Thomas Telford School

Wind

The sun shone brightly yet the air blew hard and loud,
Whipping round all the trees the air hissed and blew,
Scattering all the autumn leaves with a light rustle,
Whirling, whooshing round the bends,
Swish, swoosh surely it could not be the end,
The wind invisible, but strong,
Trails through the tunnel in a heavy breeze.
The wind will never tire and will always be heard.

Jaspal Virdee (11)
Thomas Telford School

Walking Dead

Here we are, marching to our death
The noise sending chills through our spines
Like cattle for the slaughter.
Here we are, marching to our death.

Here we are, all as one
Silently marching on.
The deafening silence awaits,
Thoughts of the family we are leaving behind
And of looking down on them from above,
Here we are, all as one.

Here we are, near our final destination,
Guns firing, the sound piercing our souls.
Stars being resurrected in the night sky,
The moon looking down with pity.
Shouting coming from in front and behind,
Just muffles in our ears.
Guns still firing, men still falling,
The time has come,
For the final breath
And here we are, at our final destination.

Emma Davies (14)
Thomas Telford School

Autumn

By the gate I stand and feel
The wind blowing through my hair,
Watching the leaves falling off the trees,
Making all the branches bare.

Along the amber carpets I walk,
Kicking up all the leaves,
All warm in my coat, I'm laughing inside
Thinking of the butt naked trees.

Gemma Hedges (13)
Thomas Telford School

The Soldier

The soldier marches, to be rid of his sins,
For he has done some terrible things.
Shooting and bombing,
His work is ongoing,
Shooting and killing
Lots of blood spilling.
All from the small turret of a gun,
But still his work goes undone.
He asks questions of himself
Hiding his emotions up on a shelf.
'When will this nightmare end?
In the army, there is no time for a friend!'
Thoughts of peace rushing round his head,
Now he dreams that he is dead,
In some of his dreams.
Something had stopped the screams,
The fighting was over.
Sunrays lighting
For the war was over.
A pat on the shoulder.
But all a dream.
For the same routine
Would start all over
One more soldier.

Stuart Pearson (13)
Thomas Telford School

Ice Skating

Cutting through the ice,
The blades slip slowly, steadily,
Tickling the ice.

Shawnee Blackmore (11)
Thomas Telford School

Forty Winks

All the loud sounds seem quiet.
Lamp posts and trees multiply again and again
Slowly the image in front of you turns to a blur
And it's like an iron press slowly pushing down on your eyelids
Eventually there is sudden darkness
Everything is quiet.

Perpetual twilight.
Streams of light flash in front of your eyes.
Two different colours spread out and turn into a small maze.
You enter it and the colours around lead into a hole.
Suddenly the iron press is turned off
You experience a shock and a shudder,

But your experience is short like your first dream
You return through the vortex and into a perplexing dimension
Of lights and nonsense
Deep sleep. You're as deaf as a post and as blind as a bat
But then a muffled sound gets louder and clearer then wakes you up
'What was that?' you ask.
It was the sound of a horn from a car.

You are travelling at speeds of over 100 miles per hour.
You quickly look behind at your children
And across to your wife. All asleep.
Too late, this all happens in a couple of seconds.
Just ten seconds after your warning you crash into the central barrier

The seats swallowed your family whole
Then suddenly flew back like when a parachute is released
Children fly through the windscreen,
The woman hits her head on the dashboard
And you witness a nightmare which is your fault.
Something you could have controlled, now you can't control a thing.
You and your family have experienced a terrible death.

Pavan Manak (13)
Thomas Telford School

Winter Poem

Snowflakes fall from out of sight
And cover the ground in the whitest of white,
The weather turns from warm to cool
When the children break up from school.
Winter's the best time of year
It's always full of joy and cheer.

Build a snowman with a mate
Find a frozen pond and skate,
A snowball fight, what a fun lark,
But winter days are often dark.
Winter's the best time of year
It's always full of joy and cheer.

The Christmas tree will then arrive
And bring the house back alive,
Using up the winter store,
Carol singers, door to door.
Winter's the best time of year,
It's always full of joy and cheer.

If the children make no noise,
Their stockings will be filled with toys.
Presents are unwrapped with haste,
Dinner leaves a lovely taste.
Winter's the best time of year,
It's always full of joy and cheer.

After Christmas has gone,
There has been fun for everyone,
The New Year is about to start,
And everyone is full of heart.
We welcome in the New Year,
Let's hope that it's full of joy and cheer.

Alex Humphreys (13)
Thomas Telford School

Shadows

Stalking me everywhere,
Copying my every move,
Just watching me, watching
And waiting with long, black, spidery fingers
Groping across my wall
At night, as the wind howls
And the trees hide from the wind,
Trying to scare me.

I walk along the street and he follows,
I stand still and so does he,
I run and he runs at the same speed,
He stalks me everywhere like a crazed person
Doing whatever I do.

Scaring little children,
Watching everyone
Stalking everyone
Just watching us wherever we go.

Jason Barlow (14)
Thomas Telford School

Winter

The year was dying in cold blue light
Frost blanketed the ground during the night
Cherry-lipped children with roses on their cheeks
Sunken-eyed players, wrapped in layers for weeks
Rock-hard water shines in the sun
No swimming in the water, but sliding's just as fun.

Days getting faster, nights going slower
Sun losing heat, moving over us lower
Trees naked, leafless, swaying in the breeze
Dear people slipping, falling on icy freeze
The year died, nature slept
Safe beneath snow's protection kept.

Daniel Bate (13)
Thomas Telford School

My Alien Poem

I live in the attic
I come from the planet Vance
My special ability is morphing
My alien name is Lance
I've haunted the attic for hundreds of years
My height twelve foot tall
My diet is worms for breakfast
I've two eyes shaped like beetles
Two long toes like snakes
My body is made out of rubber
The colours are blue and black
My two legs are as thin as twigs
My skull is naked
I have no nose
I live in the attic
Nobody knows.

Elliott Forrester (13)
Thomas Telford School

Autumn To Me

All the leaves falling down from the trees,
Under the conker tree I stand,
The different colours, the reds, browns and oranges,
The wind growling as if it was a lion,
Tonight, I will be all toasty and warm in my bed,
Autumn good morning,
Summer goodnight!

Blackberries growing along the canal,
Under the arched bridge I stand,
The water getting colder by the day,
Gently swirling around the rushes,
Tonight I will be cosy and warm in my bed,
Autumn good morning,
Summer goodbye!

Emma Clarke (12)
Thomas Telford School

Serafina The Spider

In the attic, where I live,
I'm the centre of attention,
I'm as big as a boulder,
But the thing I most like to mention,
Is that I'm as sweet as a swimming pool,
Filled to the top with strawberry jelly,
I have a cuisine of mashed fly liver every day,
For the sake of my belly.

I am like a courageous lion,
I could measure up to one any day,
With their cuddly, silky coat,
All the animals would come and pay,
Respect to me and all my goodwill,
Like the darkness in the attic that all day,
Hugs and shrouds me in soft, warm kisses.
Because it loves me in a special way.

Everyone adores me,
But it's no surprise really,
I'm as irresistible as a newborn kitten,
And anyone would be silly,
To not call me 'Your Highness',
I'm the best spider in the world or anywhere!
But how would I know?
(Because there is no one in there!)

Katherine James (11)
Thomas Telford School

A Performance By Mother Nature

I heard the growl from far away
And saw the long grasses among the fields
Begin to run, roll and race in the howling wind.

The small, fluffy, friendly clouds
Were pushed aside and cleared
Away by the *big boys!*
Who stirred up anger deep inside.

I heard the crack and felt the fright,
This was real, there was no fake.
Mother Nature was shedding her anger across the plain
And echoed her tormenting outcry
Amongst the peaks of the mountains.

There was no chance, no stopping her,
Like a clawed hand she reached down
To bless her ground on Earth with bloodshed and terror.

She moaned a mental cry
And like a thousand war planes
Bombing over the torn horizon
She crashed down her lightning forks
And slowly, she gracefully exited her performance off the stage,
But from her first grumble to her last roar,
I knew that she would return, to come out and play.

Sarah Stowe (13)
Thomas Telford School

My First Day Of School

I can't describe where I was,
I had never been there before.
I was curious,
Ever since I walked through that door.

They stared at me,
I don't know why.
I looked at my feet
And then the sky.

I looked at the other kids,
I just about managed a smile.
I sat down by myself,
They still stared for quite a while.

I don't know what,
I can't describe,
A room full of strangers,
Each with something to hide.

I looked around the room,
I saw a lot of shapes that day.
I wanted to speak.
But I had nothing to say.

'So how was your first school day?'
I knew where I was, unlike before.
I was reassured.
Ever since I walked out that door.

Riccardo Colabella (13)
Thomas Telford School

The Park

The swing, swaying slowly in the light breeze,
The whispering, whistling, wind-shaken trees.
The teens have long gone leaving the wind on its own,
Till the light comes back and the children well known,
Will come rushing back.
The vandalised swings and the broken slide,
As if someone had jumped off, trying to glide.
The darkness brought doom, destruction and death,
Not to this place, it's silent, still, almost sad.

Then the dark gives way to the long awaited, luminous light.
The trees stop whispering and whistling.
The young, rosy, red-faced children come flooding back.
The still, silent place is now transformed
To a howling, happy, hooraying herd of unruly kids.
The damage done to the place that looked so bad last time
Now looks new, no damage shows up.
The kids now leave and make way for the teens.
Armed with spray paint and cigs
They viciously, violently vandalise the place
Seriously violating the rules.

When they go back from whence they came
Once again the still, silent site comes back
Once again the willows whisper and whistle as if talking to each other.
Waiting for the kids to come back again
So the cycle of the playground starts once more.

Peter Willett (11)
Thomas Telford School

From The Planet Jupiter

My name is Emporous,
From the planet of Jupiter,
I'm sitting in a cereal box,
On the table, of a family on Earth.

I'm thinking of how they'd scream,
How they'd positively bring down the house,
If they'd just open my cereal box,
So I can finally get out.

Just imagine their putrid reaction,
As they would see my scaly skin
And observe that I, unlike them,
Have no head at the top.

The would go oh so pale,
As they looked upon my 21 arms
Beholding my oily, round torso,
Above my wide, oblong-shaped waist.

Cringing they would perceive my legs,
All 214, the width of hairs
And taking in my long, lank neck,
Which sprouts out of my waist.

Looking towards the end of my neck,
They would come across my head,
A round shape, wrinkly and black,
In the middle a single withered hole.

But for now I'll just have to wait
And imagine the scene again,
Until they *do* open up my box
And find out what's in store!

Philip Liebman (12)
Thomas Telford School

Feeling And Meanings

Are your feelings really in your heart,
Or are they just thoughts in your head?
I feel like there's a deep, dark aching
Just underneath my ribcage,
Yet I don't know the cause.

I end up deep in thought
And almost start to cry
But then I realise, I realise
I'm not actually thinking about anything.

I'm staring, sighing, sleeping and waking
But yet there is still emptiness inside,
My life is a clock ticking round
Round with no change until the batteries run out.

I look in the mirror for hours on end
Not because I'm conceited
But because I'm trying to figure out,
Figure out if what stares back at me -
Is what other people see.

But then again does it really matter -
What other people see - that is?
No it doesn't, not to me!
Because no matter what people think

I still feel the same deep emptiness
With no meaning, reason or thought
to go with it
Just tears.

Tonika Martin (14)
Thomas Telford School

A Funeral

As the hearse drove up,
I felt pain stabbing into me.
The welcoming shout was
The only thing important.
The door opened and time slowed,
I felt warmth, he was alive!
The last moments I had with him
Would never be forgotten.

He bounded happily, into his coffin,
The restraining rope was attached,
But that didn't stop him.
He jumped up to see
His home disappearing
And his family mourning.

Josh Poole (13)
Thomas Telford School

A Plane

They fill him up
Until there is no room left,
But still he rumbles,
Shaking so hard he jumps off the floor

And glides over the hills and mountain tops,
Tucking himself in, he races faster and faster,
Sliding and swishing smoothly from home to home
He's like a bird but never flaps his wings.

Wide eyes follow the trail he leaves,
As he whooshes past with a puff.
Just like magic he will disappear,
But seconds later pops out again.

His whole body seems to emerge,
As he dives head first towards the ground.
Rattling along until he comes to a complete stop
And the process starts over again.

Victoria Hargrove (13)
Thomas Telford School

The Rocks

The rocks glistened in the sunlight,
As little raindrops glistened down on them.
The jagged rocks were like teeth,
With their unsmooth edges and their wavy ends.
The smooth, silky sopping rocks seemed to say something,
'Do not touch me or else.'
This warning was taken by many passing by,
But some ignored this and carried on.

Today the rocks sit all alone.
They have no visitors as they are old and ruined,
But these rocks have more than just outer beauty.
These rocks have history,
These rocks have inner beauty.
If only someone had cared,
If only life wasn't so harsh.

Jonathan Whiting (13)
Thomas Telford School

The Unicorn

The unicorn glistened on the land,
He shimmered on the Earth,
Waiting for another of his kind,
With the moon that shone in the sky,
The stars reflected off his fur,
All silvery, pure light.
His mane was soft and shiny,
Flowing in the wind.
His head up,
Proud of his strength,
Yet his legs were firm and strong.
Holding his body, running along.
His horn was like a spear,
Pointing towards his destiny.

Helene Goransson (11)
Thomas Telford School

Old Age

It's funny how old age suddenly appears,
Like a leech to suck away your youth,
First wrinkles appear,
Like waves to lap up the smooth skin.
Then you start becoming deaf,
As deaf as a door post
And then of course you start to become less and less active,
Like a dog that has been paralysed but,

Then the final stage is that you die,
Like a rose that has withered away.
It is really sad, old age.

The thing is to eat healthily
And not to smoke
Otherwise, you will die before you get old
And that isn't good at all.

After you die you will go up to Heaven
And then *bang!* The process starts all over again.
So really it is good to die because you go up to Heaven,
So there isn't anything to worry about, right?

Matthew Spruce (13)
Thomas Telford School

My War Poem

Planes overhead with bellowing engines,
Leaving trails of warpath and pain.
But we ignore and eat our rations out of mouldy tins,
We're losing the plot, causing soldiers to be forced insane.

We trundle through mud as cold as ice,
Our colony of troops decrease, no hope in sight,
People feeling low and so I offer generous advice,
It's getting dark now, I hope I will survive the deadly night.

Sukhdeep Sarai (13)
Thomas Telford School

Seasons

Spring is when the flowers begin to bloom,
Winter is when it turns to gloom,
Summer is all happy and bright,
Autumn is when it turns colder at night.

Now we are in the season of spring,
The wedding bells start to ring,
Flowers start to sprout
And the birds begin to shout.

Summer comes next, all warm and bright,
It stays light, very late at night,
The sky becomes blue,
Children are splashing in the sea too.

Autumn is full of colours, red, orange and brown,
The brightness of the day starts to turn down,
Leaves start to fall off the trees,
Here comes the winter breeze.

Winter is here at last,
Summer is in the past,
The winter wind starts to blow,
But the children still happily play in the snow.

Laura Glaze (13)
Thomas Telford School

The Park

In the summer, the park is full of children,
Adults and babies, screaming, wailing,
The sound of rusty swings,
The sight of the sun's rays,
Shining, shining.

In the winter the park is silent and empty,
Except for the sound of intrusion from the rain,
The slide is slippier, slidier.

Jade Gutteridge (11)
Thomas Telford School

The Red Angels Of The Country

I sit watching them as they skulk along the hedgerows,
Their bushy tails wavering in the wind as they prick their ears
and listen to the noise of the countryside,
The soft padding of their paws is almost silent in the hustle
and bustle of yellowhammers in the hedges,
And then when you look into their deep brown eyes you slowly
unravel the problems of this secretive angel of the woods
and fields.
The speed of the chase and the barking of the hounds calling
for your blood,
The whinnying of the horses as they pound away at the land
with their eyes red with bloodlust,
The men with their rifles that lash out suddenly at the first
sign of red fur.
The image of this ruthless sport in your head makes you think
why would anyone want to hunt and kill something so beautiful
for sport?
It makes you wonder how low people can sink if they get their
thrills from shooting such beautiful creatures.

Xander Berkeley (13)
Thomas Telford School

Autumn

The smell of burning firewood,
The smell of evergreen trees,
As I walk through the wood,
Crunching on the crisp, dry leaves.

The taste of hot chocolate trickling down my throat,
After a warm Sunday dinner with my family.

The sight of sparkling fireworks, red, green and blue,
Flying up in the air, with little sparkles
Landing on the ground beside me.

I listen to the squirrels playing around in the golden-brown leaves,
Rustling through them to find food.

Tiffany Mallen (12)
Thomas Telford School

The Nightclub Of Sound

Silence,
No one is around
To make a sound
Not even a cleaner.
Silence
There's not even a mouse
In that house
Only silence is in there.

As the sun goes down
Out comes the town
For a few drinks and a laugh.

Noise
There are people around
To make some sound
Noise
The mice have been scared off
By the rock and pop music
Soon only rubbish will be left in there.

Natalie Plant (12)
Thomas Telford School

Put Down

Put down your axes and mantles
Give the fiery tongues a rest
Harsh words will lead to suffering
You'll find this isn't best

Put down your new legislation
That make the poor men cry
Put down your great reputations
And slowly ask yourself, *why?*

Put down the bomb or the bullet
And choose to not load the gun
If you can put down the temper
Then you, my friend, have won.

Bethan Casinelli (13)
Thomas Telford School

Horse Whisper

Slowly as the dark wind blows,
The horses begin to rise
From the dark depths of the trees
And the great white horse neighs,
'Watch out my friends, watch out,
The hunter's steps are close,
For if he shoots you with his gun
To Heaven you will go.'

As he speaks a gunshot sounds
And the birds begin to fly.
For it is the hunter.

Off the horses gallop as stars fall
And day begins to rise
For the hunter shall carry guilt with him
For shooting nature's pride.

Abigail Cooper (11)
Thomas Telford School

Autumn In The Forest

By day the forest is an enchanting place,
Warm autumn sun shines high in the clear blue sky
Frost glistening on the bare branches
Golden brown leaves floating silently to the ground
Swirling and whirling in the crisp icy breeze
Squirrels are playing, scurrying from tree to tree
Munching and crunching on acorns and conkers we see.

As night falls the forest takes on an eerie face
Darkness enfolds the ground like a witch's cape
The moonlight glows from the blackened sky
And stars look down like a thousand eyes
A lone owl hoots, night-time is here
The forest is now a place to fear.

Daniel Bosi (12)
Thomas Telford School

The Tree

There it stood full of life,
Delicate green leaves framing cherry blossom,
Sunlight warming its slender branches,
Newborn children blooming like buds of a flower.

The great tree grew
Birds hopping on now strong branches, reaching out for more life
The growing cherry blossom in full bloom
Fluttering in the summer breeze.

As the summer draws to an end
The leaves say their last goodbye
Yellow, orange, gold and brown
The children crunch them into dust.

The bare tree stands alone
The bitter cold envelops the tree
And young adults wander by
Watching their children play in the snow.

Laura Morris (13)
Thomas Telford School

Graveyard

During the day,
Sounds of weeping,
Sounds of the spade hitting the earth,
Sounds of relatives gently talking to their loved ones,
The hearse going over the gravel path - *crunch, crunch!*
Chirping birds, chirping cheerfully.

But at night,
Rustling leaves,
Owls hooting,
Dogs barking,
Whistling winds
And then . . .
Silence.

James Muir (11)
Thomas Telford School

Snow Leopard

The snow leopard's fur as soft as fleece on a newborn lamb,
With his giant paws crunching on the crisp cold snow,
As he glides silently over the frozen land,
In the depth of the winter's night.

When the beams of the full moon like fingers of light,
Strike him to make a powerful, strong shadow,
Then the hunting begins,
Where shall he strike? Nobody knows.

The cool air from the moonlit sky gently sways his whiskers,
As he searches for his victims of prey,
He attacks with his claws as sharp as razors,
That penetrate the prey like a needle through cloth.

Patiently he waits for his prey to submit,
Then he carries his trophy triumphantly back to his lair,
Satisfied once again,
He shall return to the shadows for another day.

When the animals awaken in the morning
They see the bloodstained snow and start to follow,
They see the peaceful killer
Sleeping on its own in the shadows of his lair.

Emma Sutton (11)
Thomas Telford School

India

India is orange
India is hot like summer
India is a tough wrestler
India is a sun
India is a sari
India is a sofa, nice and soft
India is like EastEnders, full of action
India is a spicy chicken curry.

Amandip Ajimal (11)
Thomas Telford School

All Hallows Eve

Clanking chains
And creaking stairs,
Ghosts that catch you
Unawares.

Witches, warlocks,
Vampires, bats,
Ghouls and ghosties,
Spooky hats.

Pumpkins burning,
Their eyes so bright,
Black cats slinking
Out of sight.

Graveyards,
Stories read
By candlelight,
All these things give you a *fright!*

Amy Stevens (12)
Thomas Telford School

The Shark

The shark is a fierce predator
And makes its own race flee,
And is a red-hot radiator
To all the fish in the sea.
He slips on his blue coat
And swims dangerously around his moat,
He is like vindaloo creeping down your neck
And when you're on a ship you will be on top deck.
The shark rushes through the black ocean
Trying to find some source of motion,
And this is how the shark destroys lives
By taking a deadly deep blue dive.

Ben Lewis (11)
Thomas Telford School

Life's Lie

All alone,
up above,
in the clouds,
I hear the click,
the wail of death.

What is the point?
I ask myself.
Why do we take the lives of the innocent,
by the say-so of the guilty?
Why?

The lights flash below
before they know,
it's all dark.
They cease to exist,
why do they call it the First World War?

Abby Clifford (13)
Thomas Telford School

Cats

They're warm just like a fiery red or peach,
But feel so silky to touch,
Lying there so content
Like a forgotten jacket
That is so quiet,
It's as though it has run away,
But most likely
It's gone to find his prey.

They can be quite mischievous
But have a heart as sweet as chocolate,
And the majority of them are
As clean as a whistle,
But is a pet for life,
Not just for Christmas.

Craig Abley (12)
Thomas Telford School

Winter

We prisoners feel trapped, it's hard to get out,
Standing in our own solid feet,
Suddenly you chatter away from your mouth,
Quickly, you can't stop it, you'll find it repeats.

The dog's fur so warm, he lies down silently,
While we slave away having to go outside,
The snakes are out there, leaping up at our eyes,
We start digging with our shovels and push the snakes to one side.

The days repeat themselves, we still hear the chatter,
Working away through the darkest hour,
Shovelling away our innocence and purity,
We've had enough of this, our faces turn blue and sour.

But alas, this long sentence is finally done,
No more extra chores to do over out there,
We're free to roam the world - not kept stuck inside,
For that short period of time we were the prisoners.

Katherine Welch (13)
Thomas Telford School

The Game Of War

Sometimes a shell
Sometimes it's hell
Sometimes a bullet or two
Sometimes the gas is sneaking
Trying to catch you sleeping
Sometimes a bomb or trench mortar
Sometimes a whizz, bang or two
Sometimes it's mud
Sometimes it's blood
When you play in this game
Called war.

Sarah Vernon (12)
Thomas Telford School

Alien

It squirts from the top like a bamboo blaster gun
And leaves loads of squiggly gibberish
On the sheet of white paper
It leaves shapes of all sizes
There are spaces after each joined squiggle.

Steam comes from its eyes
And a fresh turkey was put in earlier
But just now a brown one came out.

A hand held Super Mario with flying enemies
And coins to collect all in one compact games system.

A booming roar of deafening sounds
As there is a lot of speech coming out
The speech is talking to you.

The flashing lights on the box and a booming noise
Coming from around the back
The colours seem to be making some sort of pattern.

The whirlwinds of flying dirt
And the black hole of a mouth
That would eat you instantly was gaping right at you.

The blinding light and the flying saucer
Inside the mouth that would open after every beep
Had a sacrifice of food that spun
The beep came and lovely cooked food came out.

Daniel Key (12)
Thomas Telford School

There Is . . . Nothing

A flame is dancing,
Brightly and incandescently, until
Whoosh, a gust of wind and it is extinguished.

A ladybird is crawling
Merrily between the long green grass, until
Stamp, it has been buried in its grave.

A minnow is darting
Down a babbling stream, until,
The swooping of a bird, it has taken its last breath.

A dark shadow is following
And mirroring its partner, until,
The sun disappears behind a cloud, it is no more.

A young child is starting
To try and cross a road alone, until,
A screeching of brakes, it is too late.

An old man is reading
The Sunday newspaper, until,
The ticking of time, his time is done.

A generation scurrying
About their daily lives, too busy to think, until,
A few million years pass by, there is . . . nothing.

Marie Burrows (13)
Thomas Telford School

The Alien

As I sat at the back
Of the school bus
Watching the children play,
I noticed I was different
In a very special way.

With my big eyes
And green face
I looked in the window
And thought, *what a disgrace.*

All the children
Stare at me
In a funny way.
They look at my
Skinny green legs
And my very large head.

My neck is like a snake,
My fingers are like worms,
I'm know I'm different
In a very special way.
I hate this place,
I don't want to stay.

Christopher Harvey (12)
Thomas Telford School

My Alien

I was helping the young, innocent school children across the road,
But nobody knew.
I had no hair, but only baldness,
My skin was green and slimy.
There are no ears for there are only holes,
My eyes are big and yellow, full of hatred,
Watching the innocent little children go by,
Licking my three lots of lips,
But nobody knew.
My neck was as long as a giraffe's,
My arms were stretchy like elastic,
They were full of sharp red spikes,
Just like a rose bush,
They were ready to grab the innocent children,
But nobody knew.
My body was toned like a bodybuilder's,
My legs moved like a cheetah,
My feet are like boats,
The nails are like claws of an eagle,
Ready to grab an innocent little school child,
But nobody knew I was the lollipop man.

David Roberts (12)
Thomas Telford School

The Gerog

I just sit in the library,
In-between maps and French books,
Hidden behind the bookcase,
Where nobody will look.

A Gerog, like me, looks quite odd,
'Out of this world!' you might say,
If you said that you'd probably be right,
As I'm a Gerog from Teroosey.

On top of my head is an antenna,
To hear and smell the outside,
Then I have three bulbous eyes,
They can see 180° wide.

Next come down to my wide mouth,
Completely toothless and black,
I have no recognisable neck,
My head is just stuck to my back.

My long tongue can reach far out,
To pick up and move objects,
I also have a hole in my mouth,
To squirt acid jets.

The top of my body is silky and smooth,
But just look at the other side,
Covered in blue and green suction cups,
I can hang on to any ride!

At the end of my body is a long green tail,
This moves me quickly along,
I can go in any direction,
It makes sure I don't go wrong.

As I sit here in the library,
In-between maps and French books,
I wonder if anyone will ever find me,
Have they ever looked?

Neil Allard (12)
Thomas Telford School

Mother And Her Young One

Sunshine shines down on the dry land
Sand blows freely in the hot air
Very little shelters can be seen for miles
Soft noises of the living

Mother and baby lying peacefully under the large shade
The calming atmosphere relaxes the young one
Ripples in the large watering hole
Are the only noises to be heard

Mother becomes very uneasy as a unusual sound is heard
Bang! With horror the mother grabs her baby
But the baby is petrified so she hides

The mother gets faster and faster
But cannot carry on, she's forgotten her baby
She starts to run back to capture her baby
She gets nearer and can see her baby in sight

But it's too late
Bang!
She collapses to the ground
No movement
No sound

Baby appears from behind the rock
She circles her mother in worry and despair
Stillness
Silence
Bang! The baby gives a last little cry of pain
Before collapsing to the floor next to her mother

The only part connecting them together
Were their paws one on the other

But Heaven shall reunite them.

Laura Grant-Roberts (14)
Thomas Telford School

Annual Surprise

It's that time of year when Santa gets here
And the snowdrops fall to the ground
It's that time of year when the parents all cheer
C'mon children gather round
When the gifts are given
And the presents unwrapped
The children disappear to their rooms
Where they play with new toys which give them great joy
Then they fall asleep in mid-afternoon
They wake up for tea and watch some TV
Until Mum comes to put them to bed
So they crawl up the stairs and find teddy bears
Then they get into bed and rest their eyes
Now they can't wait
For next year's too late
For Santa's an annual surprise.

Ryan Groves (14)
Thomas Telford School

The Park

The sun has risen,
A deafening noise comes from the park.
The screech of the roundabout whirling round and round,
The high-pitched squeak of the swings.
Children screaming and laughing, running about,
Playing tag or kiss chase.
The stamping of feet and the rattling of wheels,
Leaving the park empty and still in the dark of the night,
The hoot of an owl, eerie, the sound of the echo.
The wind whistles through the trees,
Then giving way to the sound of the rustling leaves,
The soft sound of a cat as it tiptoes through the grass, eyes gleaming.
The darkness has invaded.

Rebecca Cox (11)
Thomas Telford School

My Alien

I'm Pinstorm,
I'm from Pluto,
It's a great planet,
But I've got no peers.

I'm in the corner of the class,
All lonely and sad.
None can see me
But I'm surely there.

My skin's like a snake's,
All scabby and dry.
My ears are like funnels,
Blowing out fire as if it were unknown.

I've got spikes on my arm
Like a hedgehog's back.
Not like yours,
All firm and soft.

I've got six eyes on either side of my head,
And they are so tremendously great.
I've got thirty-six toes and fingers
But why haven't you?

Why I've never been seen
I just don't know.
Please teacher,
I know the answer!

Paramveer Gill (12)
Thomas Telford School

White Feather

When they give out the white feathers,
You know it's time for desperate measures.
You've ignored the signs to enlist your name,
But is it really worth the shame.
You've tried to warn your friends of the great danger,
But they didn't listen, neither did the sergeant major.
You've thought about it again and again,
But then you decide to enlist your name.
Finally in the trenches, you wonder why,
Is it worth it just waiting to die?
With blood pouring from your head,
You cry out your last word, 'Mom,' now you're dead.

Rebecca Buttery (12)
Thomas Telford School

The Autumn Day

I feel fresh outside
I see a furry squirrel
I feel a bushy tail
I taste ripe blackberries

I smell burning - a bonfire
I feel a gentle breeze
I hear ticking - a woodpecker

I run in orange crispy leaves
I see rotting leaves
I watch dark, dull clouds
I feel autumn arriving.

James Hope
Woodlands School

In The Autumn Time

The trees are whooshing
as the heron
does the all-night bop
in the cool breeze
the squirrels play
under the trees
with crackling
and crunching leaves.

Ashley Anderson (13)
Woodlands School

Love

Love is like roses all over the world
It's like strawberries, sweet and nice
Love is like you and him holding hands
And having romance.

Love is like a dove singing a song
It's like you're in a daydream
You never get it wrong
It's like singing your own song.

Love is like you and him
And him and you
And it's not about anybody else
Just you and him.

So, love is beautiful, can you see?
Can you see what I mean?
Can you hear what I hear?
Eventually he'll say, 'Will you be my wife?'
And you will say, 'Yes I will.'

Amy Evans (11)
Wrockwardine Wood Arts College

Hallowe'en

A witch flying on her broomstick
With her cat in her arms
A genie in the bottle
Catching people's charms.

A vampire drinking blood
On a very spooky night
A mummy in his ribbons
Is ready to give you a fright.

If you dare to walk outside
You're sure to get a spooky ride.

The full moon comes out at dark
And makes the world all shine
So if you're careful, very careful,
Hopefully you'll be fine.

Sinead Balla (11)
Wrockwardine Wood Arts College

Lion

Yellow lion that is like the sun
Runs like a cheetah
When it is getting chased

When the lion is hungry for his food
He roars like the thunder
And all the animals get scared
And run to their homes.

Their teeth are as sharp as a knife
Which they kill other animals with
And get their food.

His cloudy mane
Covering his face
That makes him look even scarier.

Amritpal Dhillon (11)
Wrockwardine Wood Arts College

Hocus Pocus

Witches, witches around a pot
Monkeys' blood and dinosaur snot
Disgusting things go in the pot
(Double, double, cauldrons bubble
Fire burns, it's time for trouble.)

It's a disgusting thing
When wicked witches dance they sing around the pot
They catch some frogs and kill the lot
Because disgusting things go in the pot
(Double, double, cauldrons bubble
Fire burns, it's time for trouble.)

Eye of toad and dead man's toe
Let's catch some cats, so here we go
Witches, witches, kids for tea
I'm in the witch's cupboard, oops pardon me!

Jamie Fletcher (11)
Wrockwardine Wood Arts College

A Jungle Paradise

Deep in the deadly jungle
All the animals are in a jumble
There's one animal that thinks he's funky
And that's the cheeky monkey
One animal thinks he's fat
And that's the tiny bat
There's an animal that thinks he's cool
But he's just a fool
Soon the night came near
All the animals sighed, 'Oh dear!'
The jungle animals went to bed
And the jungle became dead.

Jak Renshaw (11)
Wrockwardine Wood Arts College

My Dog

My dog is brown like caramel,
He is also black like the night sky,
He pants for water when he's hot,
He scratches himself sometimes,
He runs like a pouncing horse,
With his tail up in the air.

My dog is called Jake,
He is a German shepherd breed,
He barks when somebody's at the door,
He yelps when somebody stands on him, like his tail,
By accident of course,
Jake has earned his bronze, silver and gold award,
He is trained to be off the lead in an open field,
And when he is called he comes back.

My dog loves some attention,
He is a medium-haired German shepherd,
He rolls over onto his back and so we stroke his belly.

Rachael Pugh (11)
Wrockwardine Wood Arts College

The Darkest Night

As the sun slowly sits in its bed,
The darkest night starts to appear.
With wolves howling and cats roaming the streets,
As a full moon brightly shines down,
Whilst the whistling wind blows the trees rapidly,
When the blind bats hiding in the trees start to screech,
As the sun softly and slowly rises above.

Suzannah Palfrey (11)
Wrockwardine Wood Arts College

I Wonder

I'm walking down the street,
Looking at the clouds,
Wondering, are the clouds evaporating water,
Or are they ghosts?

I wonder, do they look after us,
Or do they give us warnings?
I see the different colours in the sky,
Reds, pinks, purples and oranges,
They could be moods, but they're nice colours.

I wonder what they are?
Big white clouds looking over us,
I would like to know what they are,
If they're interesting or are they souls?

I think what I think,
And you think what you think,
And ghosts too, they think.

Andrew Fitzgerald (12)
Wrockwardine Wood Arts College

My Dog

Black like the dark night
And white like the fresh snow
Small like a little mouse
Creeping in the hallway.

Barks like a nasty lion roaring
Snores like grumbling thunder
In the dark night.

The night turns to morning
And the morning turns to the creepy night
It starts all over again.

Laura Fletcher (11)
Wrockwardine Wood Arts College

The Sounds Of The World

Waves crashing
Drums bashing
Babies crying
Wolves dying
Children writing
Adults inviting
Party time
Out of line
Grass is growing
Nans are sewing
Girls are dancing
Balls are bouncing
Boys are playing
Teachers are saying
Angels are singing
J-Lo is blinging
People riding bikes
She's saying she likes
Whales splashing
Yellow and blue clashing
I said hi
I'm saying goodbye.

Kelly Whitehead (11)
Wrockwardine Wood Arts College

Sounds

Sounds, sounds everywhere
In the ground and in the air
Sounds are loud, sounds are soft
You might hear some up in the loft.

Some are from birds
Some are from herds
Some are from children screaming
Some are from people gleaming.

Some are helpful, some are not
You might want some tea in the pot
Helpful ones are the radio tune
The annoying ones are the rattle of the spoons.

Hear the raindrops
Dripping on the rooftops
It's not just the raindrops, it's the rustle of trees
So come and hear, come and see.

Sounds, sounds everywhere
In the ground and in the air
Drip, drip, drip on the rooftop it goes
It sounds there when it snows.

Samantha Wormstone (11)
Wrockwardine Wood Arts College

Another School Day

I wake up every morning
Dreading going to school
But the thing I keep forgetting
Is all the school rules!

I have my breakfast, get myself washed
I feel like I'm gonna faint
I don't feel like doing today's lessons
And worst of all, I've got to paint.

I run to school quickly
I'm running out of time
I've forgot my English book
And we need it to do a rhyme.

I've got to school
It's actually going quite well
But tomorrow will always be
Another school hell!

Luke Brisco (11)
Wrockwardine Wood Arts College

My Little Brother

I've got a little brother
On his birthday he was four
He climbs the stairs and rides his bike
And even opens the door.

He is sometimes very naughty
We think he's quite a pain
But when he's tucked up in his bed
We like him once again.

Simon Trower (11)
Wrockwardine Wood Arts College